"Oh, No! I've Become *My* MOTHER"

How to outwit the "Mom Gene" and have the life *YOU* want

SANDRA REISHUS, M.H.S.

McGraw·Hill

New York   Chicago   San Francisco   Lisbon   London   Madrid   Mexico City
Milan   New Delhi   San Juan   Seoul   Singapore   Sydney   Toronto

The **McGraw·Hill** Companies

Library of Congress Cataloging-in-Publication Data

Reishus, Sandra.
    "Oh, no! I've become my mother" : how to outwit the "mom gene" and have
    the life you want / Sandra Reishus.— 1st ed.
        p.   cm.
    ISBN 0-07-144722-9
        1. Mothers and daughters.   2. Mother and child.   3. Conduct of life.
    I. Title.

    HQ755.86.R45   2006
    646.7'0085'4—dc22   2005007220

1 2 3 4 5 6 7 8 9 0   FGR/FGR   0 9 8 7 6 5

ISBN 0-07-144722-9

McGraw-Hill books are available at special quantity discounts to use as premiums and
sales promotions, or for use in corporate training programs. For more information, please
write to the Director of Special Sales, Professional Publishing, McGraw-Hill, Two Penn
Plaza, New York, NY 10121-2298. Or contact your local bookstore.

This book is printed on acid-free paper.

To Richard

With more thanks than this lifetime can hold

Contents

Acknowledgments

So many people have a hand in getting a book written and published, and I am fortunate to have been associated with many wonderful, talented people. Elizabeth Zack was there when I needed her to assist me with not only her editing skills but also her words of encouragement exactly when I needed them. She knew the book would be published from the initial writing and never wavered in her opinion. You were right, Elizabeth.

My agent, Joelle Delbourgo, was a godsend. She also believed in the book and made it a goal to get it out there for all to read. Thanks for all your work. You're an angel, Joelle.

My editor at McGraw-Hill, Michele Pezzuti, was a delight to work with. She always knew the right word to make my point even clearer, and her additions and subtractions made the book that much better. Her enthusiasm for the project was unmatchable and much appreciated. My heartfelt thanks go to you, Michele, for all your hard work and for sharing your editing gene with me, as I learned a lot. You're the best.

Thanks to my son, David Ford, for being such a wonderful son and also a great friend. I have been blessed to have you as part of my life. You are always there with your kindness along with your interest and enthusiasm for my successes, which have added great significance to them. You are truly a very special person, and I love you.

My granddaughter, Hailey Margaret Ford-Kanowsky, is my Soul Sister extraordinaire. Thanks, Hailey, for the nice person you are, the laughs we've shared, our "girl time" together, the mutual confidences, and simply for sharing you with me. Soul Sisters forever!

Thanks go to my friend and jazz dance teacher, Ron Cisneros, who has kept my body in shape for the past twenty-three years and allowed me an outlet for this part of my creativity. I appreciate the opportunities to stretch myself in a variety of ways and that you are always there for me as a dancer and as a person.

Mark Nelson-Novak, my ballroom teacher, kept me so focused on dancing details that when I danced with him everything else faded into the background. Thanks, Mark, for the laughter we share and for encouraging and supporting my dancing.

Marianne McKusick has always been so positive about everything I have undertaken. Thanks, Marianne, for all your support and a great friendship that has spanned many years.

All the people who have shared their stories with me over the years, from friends to acquaintances to clients, made this book richer. Thank you so much for your willingness to talk and your trust in me. It was appreciated then and continues to be valued now. Without you this book wouldn't have been possible.

And, last, I want to acknowledge the role my friend and mentor Ray has played in my life and offer my wholehearted thanks and gratitude to him for always believing in me and for encouraging me to reach for the stars. You made this book possible on all levels, and for that you have my undying appreciation. You are truly one of a kind.

Introduction

What woman hasn't said in total surprise—at least to herself—"I can't believe it, I'm my mother all over again"? This revelation usually comes when we are least expecting it and shocks us to the core. It can be a turn of phrase that we find ourselves using on our children, our mate, the delivery person, or that crazy driver in front of us. Maybe it's simply the tone of voice we use at that moment. Has she taken over our mind in some way? Is she more magical than we could have imagined?

Maybe we looked down at our hands and saw our mother's hands. Or maybe a sudden glance in the mirror caught a certain look in our eyes or an expression on our face that left us saying, "I'm looking at my own mother. How on earth did I get to be her?"

Nothing leaves us as offended and defensive as our mate telling us in anger that we are just like our mother. We may like Mom, but be like her? Oh please, anything but that. We saw her good points growing up, but we also saw her bad points firsthand, and we sure don't want to repeat those. We know we can do life differently, and probably even much better than she did, so for anyone to say we are just like her rattles us to our foundation.

The similarities you find between yourself and your mother, the qualities and traits she's passed on to you, I call the "mom gene." It's as if the two of you were playing a football game and she's put the ball directly into your hands. Now her characteristics are all yours to do with what you want. You get to decide if you want to hold on to them and pass them on to your children or not.

The mom gene is sitting on your shoulder influencing those areas of your life that aren't working as well as you'd like them to be. You may find your relationships less than satisfying, but you don't know why. Your sex life could be the best there is, and then again you may feel you're getting it all wrong. Getting older may not look the way you want it to, leaving you feeling gloomy about the direction your life is going, or perhaps you feel downright dismal about the prospect of living life this way forever.

You may feel depressed and unfulfilled with your life in general and know there is a better way to live, but not know how to get there or what is at the bottom of your sadness. You may be confused about your failures and choices in any area of your life and want to change, but not understand how to go about changing. How on earth did you get to where you are when you know life was supposed to turn out differently? The answers to these areas of discontent are located in the mom gene.

Even if you question the similarities between you and your mom, I can say without a doubt the likeness is there. Reading this book will help you identify what particular ways the mom gene is working in your life and eliminate the effects that are limiting you. I offer you a road map to help you get through the maze of the mother-daughter dynamic.

If you either simply ignore or completely deny the mom gene, you permit it to manipulate your life in ways you don't recognize. You can't have your own life if you are busy being Mom Jr., which is what happens before you understand the correlation between moms and daughters. This book isn't going to find you the love of your life, plop you down in the perfect job, or guarantee sexual satisfaction or graceful aging, but it will help you learn who you are and what your needs are apart from Mom's influence. It will give you tools to help locate the mom gene in your life, thus allowing you to clear the slate and re-create those areas of life that are less than happy ones for you.

Reading this book will enlighten you to Mom's ways of controlling who you are and how you live. It will help you see the parallels between yourself and your mother, then tell you how to eliminate the mom gene where you don't want it. It will show you what life can look like when you are clear about the divide that separates you from Mom.

The quest to eliminate the mom gene that influenced my own life has taken me through a very interesting labyrinth. It wasn't always easy to look at or work through, but I can now say I wouldn't have missed it for anything. The journey has freed up my life in all areas.

When I was a young child my mother and I got along fairly well, but once I hit my teenage years it wasn't always pretty. She was a strict mother who had grown up in the Midwest and then moved to the liberal, open atmosphere of California. She had a hard time letting go of her fears that someone was going to kidnap me and carry me off to Timbuktu or that I was going to be defiled in some way. My having a mind of my own and a desire for freedom didn't bode well for the two of us and led to many conflicts. She might have wanted me in by 9:00 P.M., even on weekends, but that wasn't going to work with my independent nature. If a boy and I were sitting in his car out in front of our house talking and it was 9:03, the porch light would start blinking. My mom was scared and needed to be in control, never taking into account that I was a person apart from her. The result was that I became a more rebellious teenager than I would have been if she had let me be me—within reason, of course.

Looking back now I can see that I didn't always value her opinion. Instead, I carried something inside of me that knew what I was doing and what my path in life was, which was something she couldn't comprehend. Her inability to identify with me kept the real parts of me hidden from her. We were such different people. She did eventually let up on me, and we became friendlier and had some good times together.

But my life in general wasn't satisfying me, so I decided to examine why I wasn't getting my deeper needs met. I was introduced by a therapist to the idea of Mom's influence in my life, and the breakthroughs began. What I discovered was that Mom and I got along only if I agreed with her thinking and followed her ways of operating in the world.

I could see that my relationship with my mother was hindering my freedom to become the person I knew I was supposed to be, to live the way I wanted and explore the areas that excited me. I was determined to forge a new path of independence. My life started changing and, slowly but persistently, I turned my life around. Ridding myself of the mom gene allowed me to have my own vision of my life, and my self-esteem improved. I no longer had to rely on others for my sense of self. I became more in touch with my feelings and was able to relate to others more productively. I was not only able to listen to others with an open mind, but I was also able to be clear about how I felt and to articulate my thoughts, feelings, and needs without any hidden agendas. I became more content with my life because I was living it the way that was mine alone.

I've now been able to achieve many wonderful successes and accomplish the goals I set for myself. I can see that I had to move beyond Mom's thoughts, impressions, and needs for me so I could live up to my highest potential. This book is designed to help you do the same so that you, too, can reach your highest potential and have a life that just keeps getting better and more fulfilling all the time.

In my private practice as a clinical sexologist and relationship coach I've often seen women who are stagnated by their own mom genes, and it's been a great pleasure to help them recognize and put aside those genes and start on a road of their own. They've made wonderful progress and turned their lives around, and I'm thankful I was able to assist them in their journey.

What You Can Expect from This Book

From your journey through this book you can expect help in identifying your mother's influence in your life, both positive and negative. You will learn how the mom gene got there in the first place. You will discover why Mom had this much power over you whether you voted for her to have this authority or not. You might be surprised where you find your mom in your life. Sometimes you may find the mom gene influencing you in small ways like how you laugh or drive, and other times it's more significant, like how you parent or react to criticism. If you keep walking through the steps outlined here, you will gather much insight into your mom's role in your life.

Think of Mom as a spider sitting in the middle of a web, with you, her daughter, caught and attached to her until you can break away. By reading and working with this book you will embark on a journey out of your mom's web of influence so you can have a life that is yours alone. Throughout the book there are quizzes designed to help you assess your mom gene, its hold on you, and the best ways to break free from the web. You will then be given instructions on how to release the mom gene so you can actualize your true potential. You will read stories of many women who were caught in their mother's web, some of whom got away, some who didn't, and some who are still working their way through it.

You will also learn about the many traps you can fall into unaware on your way toward independence. There's the trap of believing your mom's assessment of you is correct, the trap that if you do the opposite you aren't like your mom at all, and the denial trap. You need to know what the traps are so you can free yourself from them and be out on your own, free at last from allowing your mother—whether consciously or subconsciously—to meddle in your life. Once we've identified the mom gene and the associated traps you can fall into you will be on your way to releasing the gene from your life.

The Mom Gene and Your Relationships, Sexuality, and View of Aging

Finally we'll get to the meat of the book, which is applying all we've discovered about the mom gene to three main areas of our lives—relationships, sexuality, and aging. Even if we don't want it to be true, our mothers show up in these areas, always sitting on our shoulder, ready to show us the "right" way.

If we allow the mom gene to take over, our mothers control these regions of our lives. Knowing how the mom gene manifests and holds us back in these areas is the key to changing our lives.

Relationships

We may not think that in this day and age Mom would influence our choice of mates, but she does. She goes on our first date with us and is present all the way through the relationship. Mom taught us how to conduct our relationships—whether we want to admit it or not. I married a man who was similar to the man my mother married. Most people do that, or they marry someone just like their mother, so you can see she's not far away at all.

In Chapter 3 we meet different prototypes of mothers, and you will see how each type influences her daughter's relationships. You will learn how Mom operates and why she does what she does. If you experienced one of these moms you will see her in action and be able to say, "Ah ha, that's my mom! That's what she did with me."

After you have identified your mom and her relationship message, you will have the opportunity to look at your needs and weaknesses in the relationship sector of your life and learn steps to change the way you approach relationships so that it fits for you and you alone.

Sexuality

You would think the last place you would find Mom would be in the bedroom, but she's there also, and we as daughters are tangled in her web of involvement in our sex lives. Perhaps you only want to give sexually, but not receive; maybe sex is a chore for you; or maybe your life revolves around sex. These can be symptoms of Mom at work in your life.

Chapter 4 explains the sexual messages seven different types of moms send. Their particular influences on their daughters are explained so you can see which mom influence you have been under. Being able to identify what you were exposed to helps you recognize why your sexuality is the way it is.

Prescriptions are then given for a better, more fulfilling sexuality. Exploring your sexuality is part of the journey of discovering who you are in all areas of life, and if you are open to releasing any issues you may have picked up from Mom regarding sex, you will open the door to new pleasures that you might not have known are possible.

You can then move on to defining your own brand of sexuality. You can learn to be your own unique sex goddess—whatever that definition is for you.

View of Aging

Everything you always wanted to know about aging you learned from your mom—at least as far as she could take you. You may have fears of getting older and being dependent in one form or another. You might be ashamed you are aging in an unattractive way, feeling you are vain because you should focus on the important things in life and not on how you look or act. Perhaps you feel you have been unsuccessful in life so far by not creating the life you really wanted. These are some of the feelings that can be a direct result of Mom's mandates on aging.

Aging is not just changes your physical body goes through, but it's also a state of mind. You've heard it said that age is just a number, and that is true, but everyone experiences the feeling, and sometimes the dread, of aging. It can hit you at any age, and each age carries with it a reminder that life is moving on. You might be thrilled when you turn twenty-one because now you're seen as an adult, yet when thirty hits you wonder how you got there so fast. Forty is an age when many women have to decide if they are going to continue their life as it is and, in a sense, close up shop, or if they are going to reinvest in life and continue to grow. Each decade brings a challenge and an opportunity to look at where you are in life and decide if you are simply copying Mom or have designed your own life script.

Chapter 5 describes five aging styles to help you identify your mother's style, and goes on to show what your own healthy, productive aging can and should look like.

Now It's up to You

Without giving voice to the knowledge of past programming you will keep repeating the patterns of yesteryear, never questioning if they suit you personally or not. Once you can see that Mom's messages are not set in stone you can expand your world more than you ever thought possible.

Your ability to see the mother-daughter connection will make the difference between night and day, and this book brings to light that now life can be your personal choice. At long last, it's all up to you.

Mom's Influence on You

D ebra was driving in a rainstorm on the freeway, scared to go faster than thirty miles per hour because of all the wind and rain. Cars were whipping past her as if their drivers hadn't a care in the world. In contrast, Debra was gripping the steering wheel so tightly that her knuckles were white. Were those other drivers *crazy*? Why were they going so *fast*?

A memory suddenly came to her of a childhood summer vacation with her mother driving the family car on a mountain road so slowly that the cars and trucks behind her all started honking their horns. Her mom must have been going only twenty-five miles per hour in a forty-miles-per-hour zone. That's when the thunderbolt hit Debra: *"Oh no, I've become my mother!"* The realization made her laugh at first, but then Debra began to think about how much of her day-to-day behavior was really tied into her mother's.

The Curious World of the Mother-Daughter Relationship

Whether it hits you in your twenties, thirties, forties, or upward, the thought that you might become your mother in thought and action affects you—and every other female alive—leaving question marks in its wake. Why do I care so much what my mother thinks? Why do I never learn my lesson and know she isn't going to validate any idea I put past her? Will she ever understand me? Will she ever know I don't want unsolicited advice? Why does she always seem to sabotage me? Why will she never allow me to match up to her? Did she ever really like me? How come she can't be just my friend? The questions are endless, whether you had the most perfect mom in the world or a mother who could have played the role of the Wicked Witch of the West to perfection.

While for some women it's a pleasant thought to be like their mother, no one wants to be *exactly* like her mother. For those who truly like their mother or for those who had a less-than-wonderful mom, it's an unpleasant shock to discover that they may be repeating their mother's patterns without even realizing it. Mom's influence on an adult daughter's life is significant whether it's slightly acknowledged, fully admitted, or denied.

Why do daughters pattern their lives so much on their mother's, whether it is the same or the opposite? The answer lies in the similarity of genes, physiology, and therefore identification. Our bodies look like our mother's, and we both deal with female physical issues throughout our life: menstruation, developing breasts, sexuality, conceiving children, giving birth, and going through menopause. We either asked her how she dealt with them to get an idea of what we will face or observed how she did it. We watch how she deals with men, and we either try to copy her or do the opposite. We watch how she deals with friends and family members, how she interacts with the world at large, how she dresses, and how she talks.

Each of us has had a different experience with our mother, and we are all over the board in our feelings about her. You love your mother. You dislike your mother. You talk to her daily. You give thanks to the powers that be for caller ID so you can avoid her calls. You cherish holidays together or you make other plans. You like most of her, but there are a few things about her you would change if you had a magic wand. There are no neutral feelings about the woman who raised us. Some days we may like her, and other days she's the last person we want to even think about.

And yet, think about her we must, as our relationship with our mother was the first important one of our lives and her influence can't be denied—as much as we might like to think otherwise. Our mother conceived us, carried us, gave birth to us, and was present in our developmental years and therefore holds the keys to the way we developed. What we experienced through her helped form the perspective we have of the world and, most important, ourselves.

Mom holds this power over us because during our formative years she had the say over whether our behavior was right or wrong. She judged us and meted out rewards or punishments based on her evaluation of our good or bad behavior. This gave her the ability to try to mold us to her way of thinking, which allowed her to deem herself the expert and final judge of who we were.

This verdict was put in our heads when our brains were still forming and our reasoning powers were not yet fully developed to sort out what applied to us and what didn't. We had no choice but to allow her external input to become a law onto itself. We were at the mercy of her judgment, whether it was true or not.

We grew up thinking that Mom's belief of who we were must be true because she's the one who has known us the longest and seen us day in and day out through all our moods and changes. She must be the one who has the best picture of who we are. People on the outside may have a different vision of us, but they haven't been as close to us as Mom, so her opinion rules—whether she is right or wrong.

Mom's input became a voice sitting in judgment on our every deed, and this influence carries into our adult life. The "mom voice" lives in our heads because our mom was our first and foremost role model. When Mom is looked at from a child's perspective, she becomes the goddess showing us what women are supposed to be. In addition, according to a historical viewpoint, mothers are sacred, and we must give homage no matter what our own feelings might be about her. Added to these factors is that many of us did not learn we are a separate entity because of the web our mother spun, not letting us get too far from her, and you can see why the mom voice is so prevalent.

Our mother is our role model for being a female, whether we welcome that idea or not, and her influence is pervasive, affecting even such individual decisions as our clothing choices. My own mother loved the drama of navy and white, so for years I wore those colors, finding later that pastels were my favorites and that navy and white didn't look good on me and didn't match my personality. I felt very liberated—I had broken part of the chain that bound us unnecessarily. I was my own color guru!

When you look at your mom, take off the rose-colored glasses and put her under scrutiny the same way you put others (or at least should put others) in your life—under the microscope of compatibility. Sometimes compatibility is there and sometimes it's lacking. It's okay to like some parts of your mom and not others, and you can even dislike her if you choose. It's your life now, and you can do with it what you want. It's your turn.

For many of us, it takes more than just the fact that she's our mother for us to love our mom unreservedly and to continue the old ways of dealing with life. For others, the fact that she's our mother clouds the picture, and we put blinders on regarding her treatment of us. I have heard so many women say, "But she's my mother," excusing behaviors they wouldn't or shouldn't accept from their best friend.

Today's women are much savvier about relationships in general and want to know how and why relationships work the way they do. They turn this spotlight on their significant others, their friends, and their children and are also willing to open their eyes to their relationship with their mothers. Once we start looking at one area of our life, all other areas come under the same scrutiny. We are growing up, so to speak, and we no longer have to revere our mother just because she is our mother. It used to be sacrilegious to think our mother was anything but wonderful; today we can even laugh about her behavior with our friends and make jokes about our interactions.

But, even in the midst of this laughter, it's amazing how often the mom voice, however subtle, plays a role in our lives. We hear it in our heads almost constantly, standing guard and ready to criticize our every move, giving us unwanted advice on how we're doing in life. Usually the last place we want Mom is in our heads giving a verdict on our actions. It's enough when she's physically present, but also having to deal with her voice within us casts a shadow on our very life and makes having our own experiences sans Mom difficult.

Allowing yourself separation from this person who seemed to determine your good and bad points in childhood is imperative in your quest for your true identity. A mother who allowed and encouraged your individuality and separation from her allows you to leave the nest a confident, independent person able to survive and flourish on your own. You go out into the world able to have healthy relationships with those around you and to find satisfaction in all of your pursuits. Once you achieve this separation, you don't have Mom's voice in your head telling you that you shouldn't do that or to be fearful of the world, or that you're inadequate in some way. It's then only your own voice you hear.

It's all about separation, separation, separation and once you learn about her web and start on the road to disconnect from your mother's personal issues and live your own life, you've got the cards stacked in your favor.

That Darn Sticky Web

Imagine a spider weaving the most efficient web it can produce. It has a beautiful design, and as the light catches it you can see all the details and wonder at its splendor. Then you think about the purpose of this web—to catch sustenance with the gluelike quality of the strands. Now picture your mother as that same spider with you stuck in the adhesive. You carry the strands of Mom's web wherever you go, and those strands influence every area of your life.

The influence of Spidermom's web in your life involves many complex issues. They run the gamut from ascertaining where she ends and you begin to coming to peace with the fact that you love her, but maybe you don't like her, at least not all the time. These complex issues also include wanting to please her and at the same time wanting your own life apart from her. You are torn between allowing her to control your life and not wanting to live her life.

You want to admire her, but you may not. On some level you may want to please her, and on another level you may still be rebelling against her, and pleasing her is the last thing you want to do. This connection between mothers and daughters is a maze of contradictions, making it a web of the most intricate design. Spiders have nothing on a mother's web and could perhaps take some lessons in advanced spider web design.

It would be wonderful if her web contained only those strands showing the perfect mom; always nurturing, sweet, kind, warm, and the all-loving person Hallmark cards write about on Mother's Day. Unfortunately, that is only fantasy for the vast majority of us. Ask any woman to define the perfect mother and you will have a multitude of answers depending on the daughter's needs. Then ask that same woman if she had a mother like she described and her answer will be "Well . . . no."

For most of us, our mothers are a mixture of many different parts, some wonderful and filled with loving nurturing and other parts muddy or even dark, leaving a lot to be desired in her treatment of us as her daughter. For centuries it was almost taboo to think anything but good thoughts about one's mother, as she was perceived to hold a special place in life and was out of the range of reproach. That taboo is beginning to fall by the wayside, and we are more inclined to look at her closely to see what was positive and what was limiting or even damaging in our upbringing.

The Mom Gene Revealed

The mom gene consists of those traits of hers that you find yourself repeating. You've become your mother at that moment and lost yourself to her. Never in a million years did you think this would ever happen. Sure, you may like your mother, but become her? That is something you neither bargained for nor wanted.

Yet, when you hear her tone or words coming out of your mouth you have that moment of shock, saying to yourself, *oh no, I sound just like my mother.* You don't realize when you are growing up that those very words and beliefs are being taken in and stored for later use. You certainly didn't believe growing up that as an adult you'd be talking or thinking Mom's exact way.

How the Mom Gene Came About

Whether the mom gene came through your DNA or you had nine months in the womb as a captive audience to absorb her influence or it was passed on after you were born is debatable. Different approaches explain the mother–daughter connection in various ways.

• **Developmental psychology.** Developmental psychologists believe that parenting style is the main method for the transfer of parental characteristics to children. So, according to the developmental believers, however your mother parented you gets internalized and then you parent yourself and your children the same way. For example, if she believed you were the smartest little girl around, you would grow up believing that about yourself and pass that type of reinforcement on to your own children. On the other hand, if she always said you would never amount to anything, chances are you wouldn't and would give the same message to your own children.

• **Social learning.** Social learning models of the transmission process propose that children observe and mimic their parents' behavior. If one's parents were hypochondriacs, that becomes the norm and the children imitate that thought process and behavior. If the parents used drugs, drug use or behaviors outside society's norms become legitimized.

I see this over and over in my practice. Take the example of the military family. The children of this family don't necessarily go into a branch of the service, but the strictness and intensity in the parent or parents shows up somewhere else. Maybe the child becomes a workaholic or always fills her house with people or jogging becomes a major part of her life. The intensity will show up somewhere. This isn't always a bad thing, but it does need to be recognized to see if it indeed is working for you and not against you.

• **Behavioral genetics.** Behavioral geneticists believe that certain genes are inherited and children are preprogrammed or prewired, which explains the similarities between mothers and daughters. For example, let's say aggressiveness is a trait that is passed down to the child. This trait could be expressed in different forms such as having a bad temper, inflicting physical abuse, being hostile, engaging in self-destructive behavior, or being antagonistic. These geneticists believe that whether it's expressed toward others or oneself this trait is part of the DNA passed down to you.

A combination of all of these theories is closer to the truth. Children are influenced by the learning experience they are exposed to, the DNA passed down by their parents, and their parents' different temperaments or parenting styles. There is no cookbook formula for determining how a child is going to turn out or what a certain mother-daughter combination will look like based on just one theory.

Whatever way you arrange these variables, no matter how much a mother proclaims she loves her daughter, she has sent out messages instructing her daughter on how to repay that love, whether that way fits for her daughter or not and whether it is even warranted. Daughters try to repay their mother's love in the prescribed manner so that Mom's love doesn't go away and the daughter can feel that she's lovable and not abandoned.

If your mom didn't love and value you as a person in your own right, who ever will, since she knows you the most intimately? The message of acceptance or rejection runs deep and carries with it ramifications for all relationships in your life. A price is paid for the illusion of a mother's love that is manipulative in how you are supposed to respond. This controlling maneuver comes from the mom's need and the prescribed response should not be taken as gospel truth.

Identification with Mom

How you identified with your mother growing up is a major clue to how you function as an adult. You will adopt many of her ways of being, either if you closely identified with her or you didn't. The test is how deeply that identification is ingrained within you, which foretells how easily it can be changed. Some daughters are like their mother in temperament and outlook in life and maybe even physically look like her, which we'll talk about more in Chapter 2.

Other daughters may be the polar opposite in these areas and couldn't see themselves in their mother. Try as they might to identify with her, the identification just wasn't there and a disconnect was always present even though it may have been so deeply buried as to be unrecognizable.

Take some time remembering back to your younger years and see if you can pick out any thoughts regarding your identification with Mom. Some women I've talked to had a vague feeling growing up that they couldn't accept their mother's take on life, but pushed that thought away because she was *Mom*, for goodness' sake. Others openly acknowledged Mom was out in left field as far as they were concerned, so no emotional identification took place. Others accepted Mom lock, stock, and barrel and lived the same life as Mom. Daughter and Mom were the same person, just in different bodies.

If you as a daughter identified with your mom, her web becomes your web and her traits and perceptions become yours also. The good and bad news here is that a strong identification with Mom makes growing up easier—but you remain a shadow of her in your adult life.

If, on the other hand, you didn't have a strong identification with your mom when growing up under her care, the bad news is that you felt left out in childhood and had no role model to pattern yourself after. You were like a fish out of water. By not identifying, the good news is you are more of a clean slate once this is brought to light and addressed. Nonidentification with Mom in childhood leads you to make widespread changes that allow you to grow far beyond the family dynamics. Hooray for not fitting in—in this case at least!

MARY

Mary tried to fit in at school, with her friends, with boys, and with her family while she was growing up, but never felt she rightfully belonged in any of these areas. Nothing gave her the satisfaction of feeling she was in the right place at the right time. There was always a disconnect between what she was experiencing on the outside and what she was feeling inside. She became a cheerleader, was in the school plays, dated the cutest guy at school, and got decent grades, but nothing she did made her feel comfortable and content in her own skin.

Try as she might to find her proper place in the world, deep down inside she always felt that there was something wrong with her. She never felt understood by her family, and when she tried something that was outside of her mom's world her mother questioned her actions, always with a slight disapproval in her voice, making Mary feel even more isolated.

Since she didn't know who she really was outside of her family, her only option was to play a role in life, trying to fit in everywhere else. She was unlike her mother and couldn't identify with her but didn't know when she was growing up that it was all right for her and her mother to have a different way of seeing the world. Neither perception was right or wrong, just different.

Mothers sometimes believe their way is the right way and everything else is the wrong way, leaving their daughters to believe they are defective if they are different from the mother role they are being shown. That's where the problem came up for Mary.

Mary's mother was convinced she had all the right answers, and since Mary couldn't identify with her mom she had no one to model after and was lost in a sea of wondering, *Who am I if I don't fit in?* After much soul-searching, talking with friends, reading whatever she could find on the subject, and some therapy, Mary realized she was a person in her own right and not an extension, gene by gene, of her mother. By not identifying wholeheartedly with her mother she didn't pick up some of the dysfunction her mother had and was able to separate herself from what her mother wanted her to be and live her life on her own terms.

Mary is now a fashion model making a living at what she is good at and discredits the voice that still sometimes plays in her head saying it's wrong to be that visible. That's what her mother believed and what Mary had experienced growing up, and it was wonderful to be able to put that banner aside and know she was right where she was supposed to be in her life. She finally felt like she belonged.

If Mary had been fortunate enough to have someone by her side as she was growing up to tell her she and her mother were two very distinctly separate people and that it was okay and even normal to be different from her mother, she would have had an easier time with life.

Mary was being manipulated by Mom, but managed to go beyond Mom's reach, albeit with much struggle, as she developed a life of her own. Not everyone is willing to go through the struggle as Mary did, but if you don't you might as well hand your life to your mom on a silver platter.

The Traps That Bind

It would be wonderful if we could just shut our eyes and wish the mom gene away. If only we could simply not care what she thinks about us. If we didn't have her preconceived notion of how we are supposed to run our lives popping up all the time, life would be so much easier and we wouldn't be caught in her web. But, whether it's listening to her judgment externally or hearing her analysis internally, we all get caught in traps that tie us to Mom so that neither her inner nor outer voice is neutralized by our own separate feelings.

We put way too much stock in this voice of hers, but there is a way out and a method for silencing her unwelcome opinions. The first step is to recognize the traps and fully acknowledge their existence. Once we accomplish this step we can move forward and start eliminating these traps from our lives. But . . . first to the traps.

Some general traps keep us from getting unstuck from Mom's web so that her beliefs remain the one and only right way to do anything. Until we deal with these traps in our current way of looking at ourselves, we will be unable to take a realistic view of our lives that allows us to make conscious choices in how we want to live.

The Opposite Trap

Even if you like your mom, you don't want to be like her in all ways. If you don't like your mom, you still have picked up some of her ways of being in the world and need to recognize where and how you have done that so you can live your own independent life.

Many women I have talked to believe they have done life differently from their mom because they have done the opposite. On the surface that seems to make sense, but looking at it from a different angle you can see that if you have done the opposite of what your mom did you are still reacting to her beliefs rather than having a full spectrum of options to choose from. Either her way or the opposite way is still dealing with her view of the world. Doing the opposite of Mom will keep you tied to the mom gene, maybe forever, if you don't see the subtlety of this trap.

The "It's-All-About-Me" Trap

In the "it's-all-about-me" trap you believe that mother's assessment of you is correct because she's speaking from a place of love for you, her daughter. If only this were true. The reality is that your mother is simply another person with her own background and her reaction to her background who is now dealing with you, her daughter, through her childhood screen. Pictures from her early days with all of her anxieties, fears, doubts, and insecurities are always playing on this screen, and she relates to you through that filter, passing down her personal issues.

In the past, this passing on of issues wasn't recognized as having such a profound effect on us as it does today. Thank heavens we know it today and can separate our mother's issues from our own and know we don't have to have her blessing on each and every thing we do.

In the "it's-all-about-me" trap, we also have the mother-daughter relationship that changes over time. Where we might have pleased our mother in our younger years, the tides have changed and we can no longer seem to do anything right. This difference in our mom's treatment of us can leave us bewildered and puzzled, wondering what we did to cause this shift in our relationship. We take the responsibility for the change and believe we are not measuring up as an adult, so we try even harder to please her. We don't realize that perhaps it's not anything we did, but rather only about her needs.

The Cloudy-Vision-of-Mom Trap

At times you see Mom sharp and clear, while at other times it's as if a fog has settled in and your perception of her changes. You switch between, "She said *what?*" to "Oh, she didn't really mean it," allowing you to excuse her behavior. You can't seem to maintain a clear and steady grip on the reality of who your mother is. You waffle between thinking she is a wonderful mom and seeing all her foibles and warts.

Because you can't accept your mom's warts, you jump right back to believing in her goodness as a mom. Your vision of her is ever-changing, rendering you inadequate to sustain a realistic vision of her, or anyone else for that matter, including yourself. You are used to seeing the world and the people in it out of two separate eyes.

You close one eye and see things one way, and then you change and close the other eye and see it completely differently. If you try to look through both eyes at the same time it's like looking at a blurry screen. Nothing is clear and as a result, you are not able to hold a true picture in focus for a sustained amount of time. Instead, you bounce back and forth between opposing images of who your mother really is.

The Denial Trap

Denial can be a major problem in the mother-daughter relationship because it affects all areas of your life. Denial is almost impossible to see for those who are doing the denying, but we must uncover it or we are destined to continue down the same path that the generations of long ago established, carving even deeper ruts. Simply because something has always been done a certain way in our family makes it comfortable because we know how it feels, but that established pattern doesn't always meet our emotional, spiritual, and intellectual needs.

Most of us daughters do the opposite of Mom in some area. Perhaps we were trying to appease her and now we know in our hearts that we are our own individuals so we think we can't be anything like our mom and her view of the world. That would be great if it were true, but if you look at the bigger picture you can see that you are still operating from the perspective of her one small window into the world.

If your mom was a stay-at-home mom and you have a career, or if you get a college degree and she didn't even finish high school, or if she had twelve children and you have none you may think you are nothing like her, yet the pattern is still there. Maybe it's in the partner you choose or don't choose or in the manner in which you raise your children or your interactions with others in your life. The inherited pattern is there, and you will see it if you develop a skilled eye to view the correlation.

Anyone who denies being like her mother just might be given the shock of her life to find out that Mom was somewhere in there all along. Maybe it's not the way you thought, but she's there nonetheless. It might be in a roundabout way that you would never suspect, but releasing yourself from the denial trap requires you to take a hard look at yourself. Then you can decide if you want to change Mom's presence in your life or not.

Freeing Yourself from the Web

Discovering what works for you and you alone, separate from Mom, no matter how big or small it may be, is a freeing step in separating from Mom and being your own person with your own likes and dislikes, just as it should be.

The ideal relationship between mothers and daughters involves fusion as well as separation. The more separation our mother has allowed, coupled with the proper nurturing during this transition, the better we fare as adults with a healthy sense of ourselves. If the nurturing/separation aspect didn't happen in your case, you not only have the task of recognizing the traps, but also looking at ways to manifest your escape from the web of your mom's influence.

You can free yourself from the web if you know what to look for and work toward in your separation from your mother and her values—which may be your values also, but you'll never know that until you stand on your own, making a true division between Mom and you. The following is a start toward disconnecting yourself from her.

Devalue Mom's Opinion of You

The first step in freeing yourself is to devalue your mother's opinion of you. Remember your mom is just reacting from her past, which has nothing to do with you on a personal level. You are a different person, and no matter what view of you your mom had while you were growing up, her assessment and judgment of your worth or nonworth was not based on her ability to be objective in your regard. Even if your mom was the queen of psychology, she was still biased when it came to you.

Remember through all of her dealings with you that your mother is a product of her mother also, with all the baggage that comes with her past. She is not a clean slate able to see you for who you are. If you accept your mom's appraisal of you, sight unseen, so to speak, you have accepted an invalid conclusion of your strengths and weaknesses.

Look at Mom Through Different Eyes

To help extricate yourself from the web your mom has woven with all the erroneous messages she gave you, look at her through different eyes. See her first as a person, then as your mother. You might have had the mother who gave you birthday parties, took you to the park, walked you to your first day of school, and when you lost a tooth, put money under your pillow and said it was from the tooth fairy. She did everything a "good" mother was supposed to do. But, what did she do with your emotional needs? With the women I talk to, this is where the wonderful mother syndrome falls apart.

I was a very sensitive little girl, and I remember my mother reading me the story *The Red Shoes* and me crying at the sadness of it. My mother, being less sensitive, laughed at me and told me it was only a book and to stop crying. How wonderful it would have been, and how it would have changed my growing up, if she had stopped and asked what made me sad about the story. If she had been concerned about my feelings, we would have had a different relationship and I would have had a head start in learning to trust my emotions, rather than having to learn this through years of therapy.

Separating her as my mother from her as just another person I can see that she didn't get that type of nurturing from *her* mother. Her mother had seven children and took in ironing to make ends meet and so didn't have the time or energy to tackle her children's emotional needs. My grandmother also didn't have the skill of relating emotionally because she was raised by a cold, unfeeling aunt. My mother, following her mother's example, wasn't versed in any area except the outer and that was her limitation, which was a trait that was passed down from generation to generation.

She was my mother and I'm grateful for what she did do, but had I been shown a lineup of mothers with their disposition résumés attached, I probably would have chosen one who matched my temperament better—great skin would have been only a minor consideration, *I swear!*

Disregard Mom's Voice

When you are criticizing yourself in any way, consider whose voice you are hearing. Nine times out of ten you will find that it's your mom's, still relaying her message to you. Mom's voice can play over and over like a stuck tape, and we need to be able to identify her messages in our head as Mom visiting again and not believe the unhealthy messages she has given us. You have unconsciously internalized your mother's disapproval as your own, and it blocks you from realizing your greatest potential.

Oftentimes, just acknowledging that you are hearing your mother's voice will quiet it; at other times, you might have to be more forceful in rejecting it. You're not disrespecting your mother, but rather taking care of and mothering yourself by being the positive, supportive mom you always needed, separating her voice from your own.

Abandon the "Mother Is Sacred" Principle

Once you get past the idea that a mother is sacred and you owe her something for raising you, the notion that she is just another person gives you much more insight into both of you. You can then realistically decide what type of relationship you want to have with her, not because you owe her something but because she has a certain stance in your life. Perhaps you need to take a break from her or separate entirely or change the dynamics of your relationship so that you are an adult in your own right and your relationship with her is adult-to-adult and not still child-to-adult.

Eradicate Your Childhood Role in Her Presence

It's eerie the way some of us assume our childhood role all over again when we are in our mother's presence. All of our progress is wiped out and we become five years old again no matter if we are twenty or fifty. We all return to our assigned roles within the family until we can take the bull by the horns and make our own stand as individuals. This isn't easy, and the whole family will look at you as if aliens have messed with your head and changed you, but it's also fun to see the dynamics change, as they should. But it takes a lot of work.

Be Open to a Larger View of the World

Certainly, extremes exist on each side of the mother-daughter relationship—the most wonderful mom in the whole world or the worst mom in the universe, and there is the gray area in the middle. Not to diminish either extreme, as I know they exist, but most moms fall in the middle area. Women run the gamut in their appraisal of their mothers, and there is not a right or wrong answer here. It is up to you to take the blinders off and see your mother for who she really is, both as a mother and as a person.

Think of it as each family living with one small window into the world. Each family sees a different view from its own window, and no two look at the world in the same way. Some windows may view the tops of trees; other windows may see only feet walking by, while others face a blank wall.

If our family only sees the tops of trees, that is the only way we have to relate to the world. We may decide we are sick and tired of looking at treetops and arrange our lives to see only great bodies of water with not a treetop in sight. We've taken a different view of the world, we think, when in reality we have just done the opposite of our upbringing—not realizing there are many other ways of seeing the world as well. How about wonderful gardens or big cities or small sections of farmland or beautiful paintings or parks with children running all over? From our small window these perspectives weren't available, so as adults we have no idea they even exist, or if we have an inkling that they do, we don't know how to get there.

Problem Moms

Some types of moms stand out in their interactions with their daughters and cause issues for the daughters they claim to love. They seem to think that love is a matter of putting their own agenda forward and having everyone else fall into step with it.

To get out of the mother-daughter web, it's important to see what game your mother is playing, oftentimes unconsciously, so that you can release yourself from her web and realize it was her insecurities that built it.

The Nonseparated Mom

Many mothers hold on to their daughters for dear life and make the necessary separation difficult if not impossible. These mothers see no separation between themselves and their female child or children. Their children are mere extensions of themselves and have no life of their own in their mother's eyes. The daughter of such a mother grows up without a sense of self away from her mom.

This daughter is always doing what she thinks will bring her mom glory or a reason to be needed or validate her role as the absolute best mother ever, thereby giving meaning and purpose to her life. Sometimes daughters recognize this and work like crazy to get out of that role, while others seem to be stuck in this sticky web.

Another tactic indicative of a mom who is not separated is that she might do the opposite and try to push you into achieving what she thinks is success in the world, when you define success as something entirely different. She is simply showing a different side of the same coin, wanting you to have what she didn't have to make up for her own failings. If you can achieve what she didn't, she becomes a wonderful mom who couldn't do for herself, but could put *you* on the right path, sending her self-image through the ceiling and cementing her place in the afterworld of Special Moms.

The Jealous Mom

For a jealous mother, it was much easier to relate to you as a child because you weren't a threat to her in any way. She had the power and control, and you followed along with her wishes—pretty much at least. But as you begin to mature into an adult, all of a sudden the danger was there that you might live your life differently from how she did and that your way might be better.

The message such a mother perceives from your achievements is that she also could have lived her life differently, which is the last thing she wants to think about or acknowledge. Because she hasn't separated from her mother and then consequently from you, her daughter, she has a nagging, unrecognized feeling she somehow has not lived up to her potential.

She sees your successes through her life so that you are a mere extension of her, showing her up, in her view. She is jealous of what you have accomplished in your life because she didn't or wasn't able to achieve what you did. You might have a better job, more successful relationships, or healthier bonds with your children, and this threatens her.

Her focus is entirely on herself, and at times it's difficult to pinpoint exactly what is happening in the dynamics between the two of you. This confusion in your mother-daughter relationship can show up in a number of ways.

The jealous mom can start to resent your achievements. She may not come right out and say that she feels jealous, as she doesn't have access to the part of her that is feeling insecure about her own worth. She can't articulate her sense of unease, but she may become nitpicky, passive-aggressive, less available, or even, heaven forbid, smothering and domineering.

JULIE

Julie's mother always wanted a daughter because, she reasoned somewhere deep inside herself, she could finally get her needs met by having the type of relationship with her own child that she wasn't able to have with her mother. She expected Julie to come home from school every day and tell her everything that happened, who said and did what, and what Julie's part was in everything. She wanted a blow-by-blow description, and nothing less would satisfy her. Julie, on the other hand, was more of a private person who needed to

think things over first and even then wasn't comfortable sharing every little detail.

When Julie tried to avoid her mother's questions, her mom
made it very clear that if Julie didn't play her game, love and
attention would be withheld. To please her mother Julie had
to turn off the part of her that wasn't at ease with sharing her
deepest thoughts and feelings. She had to split off who she
really was, consequently feeling there was something inher-
ently wrong with her. Through many trials and errors, she
finally learned that, indeed, it wasn't her that had the issue in
this case, but her mother. If that was the cost of Mom's love,
maybe she didn't need it all that badly.

When mothers don't allow children to differentiate, a struggle always occurs within the child. The child doesn't know if
how she feels is right, or rather, she suspects and is led to
believe that how she feels is wrong. In Julie's case, she was so
smothered by her mother that the real Julie got lost in the shuf-
fle. If she could have stood up to her mother and not cared
what she thought, Julie would have been able to keep her own
identity. Being the quiet, sensitive person she was, however, this
was not an option for her, and she had to deal with her stolen
identity later in her life.

If you want to take a vacation staying in hostels all over Europe,
and your mother cringes at the thought of you exploring the world
on your own terms and not within a structured group, go do it anyway. You don't have to live your life through your mother's limitations to get her love—if that love is really about you and not her. If
you take the steps to break free you will eventually find great relationships with others who are on your same wavelength and live life
by what you feel inside and not with your mother choreographing
your journey through life.

Separating from Mom

Your mother may be a wonderful mom, but always remember she has her own issues to deal with and you have your own. You are not the same person no matter how similar you might be and no matter how much you look up to her. You are a creation of genes of both your mother and father and all of their ancestors, and your genes are arranged in a way that is uniquely yours. As much as your mother might like you to be exactly the daughter she always imagined having, you can't always be that for her.

Mothers today have to measure up to higher standards in the mom department than they ever have before. They can no longer rest on the laurels of the mom title but have to be open to hearing their daughter, perhaps after having been in therapy for a while, say, "Mom, there's something I'd like to talk to you about."

One mother will cringe at the words and look at a speck on the wall that she suddenly just has to get rid of, while another will say therapy is a bunch of garbage and change the subject to what just happened on her favorite TV show or what Aunt Martha found out from the doctor. The supportive mom will look at you and say, "Yes, I'd like that," inviting a discussion that will hopefully be a growing experience for both of you.

Whatever your mother's response is, it's now your turn to explore what your life path is and know it is a path that no one else has been on before. Your mother doesn't have to give you permission to be who you are, and she doesn't have to change. This is your own road and you are steering your own route.

You can learn how other people do life and how they maneuver through their own mother-daughter relationship, but in the end it's up to you to chart your own course—with or without your mother's blessing.

The beginning step toward seeing life through your own eyes and not through your mother's web is your willingness to see the connection with your mother, good, bad, or somewhere in between, pulling no punches in your appraisal of your own mother-daughter link. Step back and look at the bigger picture to see what is happening in your relationships with yourself, your children, and your parents. Look closely to find the clues that lead to a true evaluation in all these relationships.

When you are unable to see a web, you can't do anything about it, but the web design is always there—visible or not. It doesn't go away simply because you can't observe it. When the sun is shining on the web, however, all of a sudden the maze of strings is apparent to the naked eye. That's what this book does—it looks at the web from all angles as if the sun were shining on it and shows you how to finally cut the web strands connecting the two of you and leave Mom's web as hers alone. You can then move about freely on your own with no strings attached. It's wonderful being your own person! Life this way just keeps getting better and better.

2

Seeing the Picture Clearly

We've begun to explore the mysterious mother and daughter relationship and learned about some of the traps that keep us under the influence of the mom gene. Now we are going one step further to see the big picture more clearly. In this chapter you will find out how the mom gene plays out in your life. You will be asked to take a firm look at the similarities and differences between you and Mom, thus enabling you to see her gene at work in your life.

Knowing and acknowledging how Mom has influenced your life in minor as well as major ways allows you to start down the road to building your life in a new way and living it differently from how you did before. In making this major step forward, pay particular attention to the following three *Ls*.

- *Look* realistically at your mother and what you have picked up from her.
- *Listen* to the messages your mom gave you in contrast to what your inner voice is telling you.
- *Leap* into action to rid yourself of any aspect of the mom gene you deem has no value for you.

It's that easy and that hard. It took me years to get to where I feel like I'm my own person, minus any mom-gene influence that didn't work for me, and my life now looks completely different than it did all the previous years. In times past, I never thought I would be where I am today, and yet here I am.

Now you can untangle the web and uncover the memorandums about love, sex, and aging that your mother has passed on to you like the Olympic torch. You can then start to distinguish where your mom ends and you begin and gain the freedom to make your own mistakes and enjoy your own successes.

On Alert for the Mom Gene

There may be some parts of your mother you would like to emulate and others you don't want to be a part of your life. But, even if you adore your mom, you want to be your own person also. Knowledge is the key to unearthing the parts of Mom that don't fit for you, allowing you to throw off those web strands and be the person who was there underneath her web of influence all this time.

Whether the mom gene manifests itself in small or large ways doesn't matter; it's still the same mom gene, just in different degrees. It's up to you to decide if you want to continue mimicking Mom in those ways or if you want to change the way you relate to the world.

While new information regarding your mother-daughter connection may cause you to become uncomfortable, it's the only way to start moving past it. So, read and think about the statements on the following list and see how many yeses you come up with. Some of the questions are intended to help you see the minor similarities, while others address more major issues.

Mother-Daughter Awareness Scale, or
Am I My Mother?
- The older you become the more you drive like your mother.
- You pack prudently for a trip just like she did.

- You complain about your mother complaining about your father.
- You attempt to direct the lives of those close to you as your mother did with you.
- When you least expect it, you hear your mother's words and tone when you speak to your children or coworkers.
- If your mother gave up on goals, you question whether you might be doing the same thing.
- You realize you dress just like her.
- You criticize someone and think of your mom doing that to you.
- You are either thrifty or you overspend and realize she handles money the same way.
- You find yourself being judgmental and stop yourself because you sound just like your mom.
- You can admit you and Mom have the same bad temper.
- You chose a difficult romantic relationship, and it's reminiscent of your relationship with your mom.
- You have followed in your mom's career path or chosen an opposite one whether either is right or wrong for you.
- You find you have too many pairs of sensible shoes in your closet.
- As you age, you find yourself talking about all your ailments and remember how much you hated your mom talking about hers.
- You realize you eat the same foods Mom did.
- Although it didn't look like it at the beginning of the relationship, you discover down the road that your mate is critical (or condescending or withdrawn or smothering), just like the man Mom married.
- You send helpful e-mails to your children just the same as your mother used to send you articles proving her views were right all along.

What have you realized? You may find that you are like your mom in funny ways, but some behaviors are more serious and limit your individualizing. Don't panic and deny any similarities you noted in the Mother-Daughter Awareness Scale. Don't try to sentimentalize her and seemingly ignore her ways—the parts of her you didn't like growing up—because that won't help either. The key to your new beginning is to accept that you've picked up the mom gene.

Think about it this way: your mother has both good points about her—at least most mothers do—and she has parts that would never earn her high marks at the Good Mom Academy. That's the reality of the situation, and to be able to accept that you might have picked up one or two of these parts you would rather not acknowledge means you can finally separate from her. This allows you to see who your mother is as a person and, consequently, who you are as a person away from her. It's so liberating—you will feel like you've had a second chance at life, having gained a whole new perspective of you, her, and the world as you've always thought it was.

How the Mom Gene Manifests

Thinking about why you have a mom gene is helpful to some degree, but recognizing how it manifests in your life will clarify where to start on your journey toward separation. This darn gene comes out in the biggest areas of our lives, including who we pick for mates, which dictates how our closest relationships turn out, which in turn affects our entire being and vision of who we are.

The mom gene is relentless, as it also turns up in the way we age through life. As if that weren't enough, the mom gene also influences our sexuality in ways we don't even begin to know or much less want for that matter. Mom's fingerprints are all over our lives. We'll dedicate much more time later in the book to each of these topics, but right now we will take a look at how the mom gene works in our conscious and unconscious thoughts.

The Mom Gene in the Conscious and Subconscious Mind

In some aspects of your life, you know how different you are from Mom. In other facets, you may not have a clue about how you act out your mom gene, or, if you do, you have no control over it. The right hand doesn't know what the left hand is doing. This is where it gets tricky. Your conscious mind thinks one thing, and your sub-conscious mind is acting on another.

For example, you may tell yourself, and really believe in your con-scious mind, that you are a good employee, but you can't seem to get promoted at work. What the heck is going on here? Something isn't in synch, and you can't figure it out. You really want to better your situation, but you flub up all of your interviews either by being late, not being prepared, or verbally stumbling your way through those you are ready for.

Here, the two parts of the mind are working in opposite direc-tions. You may be highly qualified for the new position, but some-thing stops you from moving forward and actually getting the new job.

Perhaps you are subconsciously self-sabotaging. Maybe you are looking for the drama, or you're being punished for something you think you have done incorrectly, or maybe you're seeking sympathy and attention. Your subconscious leads you to act in a direction that is counterproductive to your conscious wants and needs for a myr-iad of reasons. You could be playing out, through your subconscious mind, messages passed down during your childhood or repeating Mom's coping mechanisms. The image of what your mother believed of the world and of you personally is stored in your emotions and therefore repeats itself, which makes it trickier to identify and sort out.

Sometimes your mother doesn't realize she has passed down these self-sabotaging behaviors, but you still act out these messages over and over. These messages can be anything from believing life isn't supposed to be easy or good to believing there's no way out of your unsatisfactory relationship because there's no rocking the boat or because you made your bed, so now you must lie in it, or believing that you aren't good enough for a new job. Maybe implementing these negative messages from Mom allows you to keep having drama in your life, which helps meet your unconscious need to focus on something other than what really needs to be addressed, just like Mom did. Or you may think you messed up that last job interview and need to be punished for it, so you repeat the destructive behaviors because it certainly was your fault, wasn't it?

Being involved in an unpleasant event often brings sympathy, which you may really need but are unsure whether you deserve it because Mom taught you to have a stiff upper lip in all matters. Perhaps you are afraid to just ask for some TLC when you feel the need for it. The subconscious mind is where all of these fears, needs, insecurities, and anxieties are stored, and this part of the mind governs much of our behavior. There is a sometimes-odd logic to the subconscious, where the mom gene hides.

But, once you get the conscious (which can be logical) and subconscious (which has a logic all its own) mind to work together it's like grabbing the brass ring on the carousel. It feels out of reach, but when you do catch it you win, and the reward is having all your parts in synch and all acting in your best interests. You become comfortable in your own skin as if someone has turned on a light inside of you that allows you to move freely in any and all situations.

But, until the logical and seemingly illogical parts of you are joined together, your subconscious mind governs your behavior. Without even recognizing why, you may act in ways that bring forth the mom gene. Look at some of your behaviors that are counter to what you say you want, and see if you are operating from your emotions, which the subconscious governs. Look at the following list and notice if you engage in any of these behaviors.

- You stay in a certain relationship when it doesn't meet your needs.
- You are an overachiever but say you want time for family or recreation.
- You yell at your children and feel bad about doing that.
- You can't allow good things to happen to you without sabotaging them.
- You accept every stray kitten, dog, bird, and person into your life.
- You want to lose weight but can't seem to do what's needed to accomplish that.
- You max out your credit cards when you know you shouldn't.
- You drink more than you should.
- You acquiesce to other's needs, putting aside your own.
- You exercise so much it becomes an obsession.
- You want to appear more intelligent, cultured, or well-read but can't seem to get from here to there.
- You are pleasant when you really want to scream.
- You overextend yourself and are tired all the time.
- You run to the doctor every other week because you are sure something is wrong.
- No matter what you do you still feel inferior to others.

If any of the above statements describes you, you are most likely operating from your emotional side, which is ruling your life. Seeing and understanding where these behaviors come from is an exciting discovery that will shed the brightest light on the confusing issue of your behavior not conforming to your desire.

Getting to the Nitty-Gritty

It's difficult to determine which mom–gene influences you've adopted and which you haven't. Even if you don't think you are anything like your mom, I guarantee the mom gene is there. The easiest way to discover which influences you've adopted is to look closely at aspects of your life. Examine the following list and answer the questions as honestly as you can.

- Do you keep friendships even when they don't work any longer to either be the same as Mom or to show her you can keep friendships when she couldn't?
- Is rebellion a way of life for you, either as it was for her or the complete opposite of the way she lived?
- If she was fearful of life, do you take risks so as not to be like her, or do you stick to the tried and true also?
- If Mom was a drama queen, do you have major dramas in your life also, or do you keep life calmingly boring?
- Do you attract "oh, woe is me" people into your life so you can fix them just like Mom did, or do you ignore everyone who comes close to being a "poor me" because Mom didn't cotton to people not handling their own issues?
- Are you living in a small box, never expanding your horizons, because Mom either did the same or went too far the other way and was out of control?

Your answers will help you spot areas where the mom gene may be lurking and may shed light on some of your behaviors. You can begin to recognize why you are the way you are and start to handpick which behaviors you want to keep and which you want to discard. It's becoming more your choice now than it has ever been in the past simply because you are seeing what comes from Mom.

These questions do not imply that you are living life incorrectly if you answered yes to them. You are finding what is working in your life and what isn't. Improving the situations and interactions in your daily life is more possible than you may realize, and you can accomplish this by simply knowing who you are apart from Mom. Removing that blasted gene allows life to just get better and better. Before we get to that, however, let's look at some of the reasons for the unhealthy gene a mother and daughter can have.

Chasms Within the Mother-Daughter Relationship

Different chasms, or gaps, are inherent in our relationship with Mom, and they should be embraced as a part of the separation process. Learning to identify our specific gaps is a major step in creating those thought processes, goals, objectives, and values that are uniquely our own.

These gaps, of which she had no control, help to explain some of our differences and difficulties with Mom. Our dissimilarities clarify why Mom saw us in one light when we were seeing a totally different light. Understanding these built-in dissimilarities and acknowledging their existence also assists us in separating from Mom.

Three such gaps are the naturally occurring generation gap, for some women the cultural gap, and last, yes, the temperament gap (personality-wise, we're not all exactly like dear old Mom!).

The Generation Gap

Every generation has a different viewpoint on the world. The young think the world is their oyster, the middle-aged often wonder what else there is, and the elderly thank God—or maybe the medical establishment—for the lives they've lived and what lies ahead of them still.

But what really factors into the mix is how different the world today is from the world in which the older generation grew up. Each generation seems to play a different ballgame. When it comes to relationships, a daughter participates in the current season with its all-new players, but Mom? She's still in the midst of last season's game.

When a mother tries to impose outdated beliefs about life, sex, and relationships on her daughter, their relationship suffers and the daughter is left without a suitable present-day coach. Life, sex, and relationships—how they present themselves and how we handle them—change as time passes, and most daughters are a product of their time, not their mother's era, which Mom seems to forget.

How a daughter is raised impacts her to a larger extent than she may realize. A daughter may subconsciously believe her mother's belief system is right (*and many times does believe just that*), so if she handles her own life in opposition to that system—usually because that's what everyone else is doing—she is plagued with guilt. After all, when daughters were growing up, they believed their mothers to be the maharishi of all knowledge.

KARI

Kari's mother, Inga, was of the old school in most aspects of life. She had a traditional marriage for her time and thought that since it was good enough for her it was good enough for Kari also. But, when the time came for Kari to think about marriage, she knew she wanted her marriage to be different than her parents'. She had grown up in a different era and had a different picture of marriage than what her mother embraced.

In her mother's generation couples accepted the expected duties of each person in the marriage—the wife inside the home and her husband on the outside. Intimacy was a foreign concept to Kari's mom and dad. They knew how to work together, but any deeper feelings and emotions were kept at bay and rarely discussed.

Kari wanted equal billing in marriage and to share responsibilities both inside and outside the home; she wanted great communication and a husband who would talk to her about feelings. When she met a sensitive, emotional, freethinking artist, she thought her dreams had come true. Introducing him to her mother was a scary proposition, however, and when Mom and the boyfriend finally met, it was distrust at first sight for both of them. Mom thought the boyfriend had been dropped down by aliens, and the boyfriend thought Mom was a relic from the dark ages.

Kari kept hearing from her mother how disastrous this relationship would be for her. Mom believed that there were certain duties of each person in a marriage and that line was not to be crossed, no matter who the two people were individually or what century they lived in. Inga was sure without a doubt that the relationship she had, and had always known relationships to be, was the only way to have a happy relationship, and Kari needed to follow in those footsteps to have a good marriage. Kari, on her side of the generation gap, was living her peers' ideal of having a shared life in all areas, and her mom's old ways didn't fit any longer.

Much to Inga's chagrin and dire warnings, Kari married her artist, only to find he was not very responsible and much too ineffectual in almost all areas for a solid relationship. He did the laundry only when *he* had nothing clean left to wear, and the dishes piled up in the sink while Kari brought in the money to live on. Kari's mom had believed her ideas were correct and wanted Kari to live her way—forgetting to factor in the different generation her daughter was growing up in and how relationships had changed during the years.

Kari's mom wanted a certain type of man for her, while Kari yearned for the complete opposite because she wanted so badly to have a different marriage from her mother. Kari knew there was a different way to have a relationship than her mother had—she just didn't know how to get there. She thought she had it figured out, but her mother's ideas still influenced her. She married the opposite, which she found out was still the same. She didn't get a man who could be emotionally close, just as Mom had not. Doing the opposite of Mom is like an image in a mirror—yes, it is the opposite of the original, but it is still an image in the same likeness.

Perhaps Kari needed a mate who was more in the middle of the two extremes, or maybe she needed to be single or, heaven forbid, first learn who she really was and what her inner self needed and not simply run off her mother's age-old relationship script, going from one extreme to the other.

Many women follow in their mother's footsteps in certain areas. They wish to support their mother, believing that if they value their mom then consequently they, the daughters, have value. Not to value their mother would reflect on their own self-image. So, daughters may get married or have children just because that's what Mom did, not even considering if that action or timing is right for them.

Too bad a wise leprechaun was not hanging around the bushes to tell these daughters it was okay to do life a different way. As it was, early in their lives this mother-value was set in stone, to be questioned and debated during adolescence for sure, but not to disappear entirely.

When faced with the generation gap, we need to realize, just as Kari did, that a mother's sage advice isn't the absolute truth. You need to experience life—and all the successes and failures that go along with it—to decide what is right for *you*. You are not just an extension of your mother's sometimes outdated beliefs, and you can come to accept this truth by recognizing that relationships, sexuality, and aging will differ from what has been acceptable in the past, simply because society itself changes with each generation. You have grown up in a society that has different expectations and values than Mom had in her day, and you have to incorporate these changes into your own life. Perhaps some parts of her advice and role modeling fit for you and maybe others don't. You don't want to follow her blindly, but you do want to look at her advice objectively and pick and choose what to keep and what to discard.

The Cultural Gap

Many women are not far removed from their immigrating ancestors. Even if the move to a new country was some generations back, parents carry forward what they learned at their mother's knee, which, in turn, their mother had learned at her mother's knee—back for many, many generations. These parents bring the cultural values of the so-called old country into the upbringing of their children. However, children born in the new country have a completely different set of morals, values, and expectations placed on them by their new culture, and the two sets don't always match.

Attempting to raise a daughter with Mom's foreign beliefs and then scolding that daughter for adopting the ways of her new world leads to a critical, judgmental environment for the daughter. From the parent's perspective, if the daughter doesn't choose the right way to live in any area of her life, the message to her is loud and clear. The error is with the daughter—certainly not with the old world ways, which have gone on since creation.

MAYA

In Maya's culture, it was expected and accepted that the parents choose the mate for their child. None of these new world ways for Maya's parents—it had been done this way for centuries and they weren't going to change now, no matter where they lived. In college, Maya met and fell in love with a young man who was not of her culture, but her mother soon intervened, and he was out the door and the man Maya's parents had chosen was brought into the picture.

From her mother's vantage point, Maya was going against the customs of her ancestors. Her mother made sure Maya knew how she was messing up her life and disrespecting the customs of her heritage by trying to make her own choice. Over and over the message was made very clear to Maya in words and actions.

The decision had nothing to do with what Maya wanted and certainly did not take into account what she felt in her heart. Her parents had decided long ago that they would choose her husband and she would make the most of it, period. It was either that or be disowned by her family. Maya's mother had indeed instilled her own cultural beliefs in her, but Maya wanted to live her own way in this new country. However, the choice was made clear—it was either her mom's way or live as an outcast from all her relatives.

Maya was left feeling that something was probably wrong with her for wanting to turn her back on tradition, so she married the man who was chosen for her. She loved her mother and wanted to do what was right—according to her mother—so as not to lose her mother's love and acceptance.

Maya was not in love with her new husband, and eventually she ended up having an affair with another man. This only added to her guilt of going against her mother's demands.

True, she did marry the man who was chosen for her but couldn't keep those vows sacred. She was rebelling against her mother and the customs of her ancestors in an indirect way.

Maya was convinced in a deep part of her that she was defective in some way because she chose infidelity and didn't comply with her mother's mandates completely. Sadly, for her this guilt took the form of health problems.

When grappling with the cultural gap, remember that it's up to you to judge if the handed-down scripts are healthy and if they are designed to give you what you really want in life. Your mother can only give you what she knows, so you must factor that into your life plan. This allows you to evaluate your life from a different perspective, and piece by piece you can build your own scripts.

Throw out the scenes that don't work and add the ones that fit for you personally. First, of course, you have to learn what scripts work in your life, and then you have to figure out how to go about getting them into your life. Following the sections on how mom experienced her relationships, sexuality, and aging in Chapters 3, 4, and 5 is information on healthier ways to live in those areas so you can get the results you desire.

The Temperament Gap

The temperament gap is the most profound and far-reaching of all and causes the most damage. While one can understand and make some peace with the generation gap and even the cultural gap, the temperament gap is not so easily recognized, overcome, or even understood by either mother or daughter.

The Merriam-Webster dictionary defines the word *temperament* as "the characteristic or habitual inclination or mode of emotional response." The *Encyclopedia Britannica* says, "In psychology, an aspect of personality concerned with emotional dispositions and reactions and their speed and intensity, the term often is used to refer to the prevailing mood or mood pattern of a person."

With these definitions in mind, take a look at the following test and see if you and your mom are afflicted by the temperament gap.

The Temperament Momometer

- Is one of you an introvert and the other an extrovert?
- Do you both gravitate to similar colors?
- Are you impatient while she has all the patience in the world or vice versa?
- Do you value her opinion on things?
- Do you have the same political or religious beliefs?
- Is one of you sensitive and the other indifferent?
- Is one of you unmoved by loud noises and does the other want only peace and quiet?
- Does one of you thrive on chaos and the other on order?
- Do you and Mom look for the same qualities when choosing friends?
- Do you both enjoy traveling to similar types of locations?
- Does one of you have high energy and the other low energy?
- Is one of you talkative and the other on the quiet side?
- Is one of you highly emotional and the other more intellectual?
- Do you both enjoy the same type of music?

The more yeses you have answered, the greater the likelihood of distancing from Mom or experiencing conflict with her. This list points out general comparisons and some of the more obvious contrasts of opposing temperaments. It is designed to make you think about the temperamental differences between you and Mom from the obvious to the more subtle ways these differences were there between the two of you. After reading and thinking about the list, assume for a moment that you and your mother did have conflicting temperaments, but she didn't know or consider the implications of the difference. For example, if you happened to have a mother who was the energetic, impatient, extroverted type and you were quiet and easygoing, and she didn't understand about different temperaments, you could have easily been labeled too passive for your own good. If it was the opposite and you were the high-energy being and she was the laid-back type of mom, you may have been tagged as being a problem child and treated accordingly.

The message was the same in either case—there was something intrinsically wrong with you. We all believe and accept our parents' opinion about who we are to some degree, and in doing so we accept the idea of the so-called flaws they decided we had. The truth could have been simply that you and your mom had different temperaments. It sounds simple, and it is, but the ramifications are in the major leagues.

If you were a sensitive and emotional child who was raised by a mom who expressed no depth of feeling, you could view yourself as too emotional and bury your sensitivity as far down as it would go. The price you pay for burying feelings during childhood is that as an adult, you attempt to deal with life on the outside while having all these unresolved feelings still inside. You have defined yourself against your mother's temperament and have lived accordingly, which prevents you from even knowing who you are standing alone. If your mom recognized a temperamental difference between the two of you and was able to honor that difference, you would have a more positive image of yourself than if she rejected the difference. Either way, there was a basic message given to you about your worth in the world.

If you do have a temperament difference with your mother, and maybe even the rest of your family, think of it as being raised by a pack of wolves. Even though you lived in the same world, you had human instincts that were different from your mother's wolf instincts. You just simply didn't understand each other or comprehend how different you two really were. You might have tried with all your might to fit in with her, and she may have tried with all her might to accept you into her world, but it just didn't work because of the differences between the two of you. Neither temperament is right or wrong, the two are just unmistakably different.

It's important to remember that you aren't wrong for having the temperament you have; it's just a matter of genetics and partly it's the environment you grew up in. If, as a baby, your genetic base was fussy because you didn't like the noise around you or active because noise didn't bother you a bit, or you were sensitive to any of the other senses, and your mother understood about temperament and molded the environment to fit you, you were accepted for your own disposition.

On the other hand, if she didn't understand and made you adjust to your surroundings no matter how you reacted to them, the environment modified your own basic temperament. How your temperament fit with your mother's and what she did with the difference determined how she treated you, which in turn gave you an image of yourself—at least through her eyes.

MONA

Mona and her mother were complete opposites. When Mona was growing up the house was always full of people. Relatives, friends, coworkers, and neighbors were always welcome, and there was an open door policy day and night. Any reason to have a party or celebration or just to visit was always greeted enthusiastically by Mona's mom. Drama was always high on her list, so along with the party atmosphere there were also crises thrown in for good measure to keep things lively and interesting.

Mona's mom would push Mona to come out and entertain the guests with her piano playing. The last thing Mona wanted to do was be in the spotlight with everyone watching her. It was worse than her first day at school. At least there others were feeling the same way and everyone was busy seeing where they fit in. Not so at home, where everyone told her how pretty she was and how she was going to be playing in Carnegie Hall one day—as if that was what she wanted.

At these times, Mona craved nothing more than to sit in her room reading or playing with her dolls. She began to say she was sick so she wouldn't have to perform for her mother's friends. Her mother didn't buy that story for a minute and scolded Mona for being so antisocial. Her mother just knew something was wrong with her daughter because she was not an overly social person and didn't like the attention. Mom was always telling Mona that these people loved her (which Mona doubted) and they wanted to hear her play, so Mona should appreciate that and rejoice in their interest.

Mona tried to please her mother, but it was at her own expense. By temperament Mona was a shy, retiring, serious person, and her desire was to be a scientist working in the field of medicine. Mom didn't understand that at all because it was contrary to who Mom was, and so she viewed Mona as lacking in some way. To her detriment, Mona internalized the verdict her mother handed down to her and assumed her mom must be right—*she was her mom, wasn't she?* She must be accurate in her appraisal.

When Mona grew up she forgot about being a scientist and landed in a job that didn't fit her, married a man who was not her intellectual equal, and had problems in her sexual life and with her choice of friends. She and her mother seemed to always be at odds. Mom couldn't understand why Mona felt so distant from her—*she had given her the most perfect road map, hadn't she?*

Mona on the other hand, couldn't understand why Mom was always criticizing her when she was just trying to be who she was. Mona couldn't be true to the person she was because of all the layers of biased judgment her mother had covered her with and so was like a ship without a rudder. Mona was simply floating through life with no direction of her own and no sense of self away from Mom's rulings about her, as much as she protested otherwise.

Life became painful and Mona felt she was floundering, so she sought the help of a therapist. She felt a connection with this person, which was a first for her, and trusted him. She learned so much about herself and the difference between herself and her mother that it changed her world. She was able to sort out herself from her mom's picture of her, and she learned she was that serious person and not a replica of her gregarious mom. Not only that, but that it was okay to be that way.

After many years of reflecting and sorting everything out, Mona is working on her science degree, has divorced her husband, is working on her sexuality and friendships, and is inching her way to having the life she envisioned for herself before Mom told her she was wrong for wanting to live her way in the world.

When this temperamental difference is the case with you and your mom, think of it as if she were looking out the right side of your small, common window and you were looking out the left side. It was the same window onto the world, but you saw the view differently based on your different temperaments. This temperamental difference determines how you fare in your mother-daughter relationship and may explain many clashes between the two of you.

When you don't get what you want out of life, the outside and inside may be working against each other. You could have been told you are a certain way, and yet you aren't that way at all; it was just a perception proclaimed by Mommy. The conflict is confusing and shows up in all areas of life. You form a relationship or follow a career path, and instead of choosing one that matches your temperament, you go against that and opt for one that doesn't let you discover who you really are under Mom's radar screen. You're playing the *Mom Says* game.

You would like to choose a mate who would encourage you to be who you really are or to find your true professional calling. But, that would take trust, and you learned long ago not to trust people and worse yet, not to trust yourself. This loss of trust was the result of knowing something on the inside and constantly being told that was not the case. You didn't know whether to trust your inner feelings and thoughts or trust what your mother told you, so you did neither. Then, since you couldn't trust yourself and you couldn't trust your parent, it left you in a quandary as to what to believe about yourself, and trust dissolved.

Now you're caught in a dilemma between believing you are wrong for being the person you are and needing to express your true nature. With this impasse, you have shut down the feeling part of yourself. What you really need to do is listen to that miniature self sitting on your shoulder whispering in your ear that you have feelings that need to be expressed.

It's quite a trap, and you can see how this plays out in all of your relationships, jobs, sexual relations, and life in general. You choose

people to be around or jobs to perform, you have a particular interaction with your children, and you have religious beliefs. All areas of
your life are affected by your mother's assessment of you. You also
deal with sexuality through this lens, and you age in a particular
manner based on the messages you received about who your mother
determined you to be. Think of your mom's assessment of you
under the heading of *The World According to Mom*. This evaluation is
just her read on you and not always the reality of who you are. You
can change your perception of yourself, but it isn't easy.

It's as if you are caught at the bottom of the Grand Canyon, looking at each side and unable to decide which wall to climb. They each
have a different terrain to cross, and you must decide where to put
your energies and your climbing rope. Do you go up the side that is
familiar and easy, believing what Mom thought about you, limiting
yourself to past ways of relating to the world, or do you climb the
unknown side, facing who you really are, facing all the uncertainty
and forging a path that is yours alone?

The unfamiliar route allows you to grow and live fully in your
own body and soul, but it takes a lot of work. The choice is yours,
but remember you must choose a side because you can't live at the
bottom of a canyon and still be a part of society. Life keeps moving,
and you move with it either by repeating the past or moving on to
newness. Knowing that you can make changes in your life helps to
overcome the effects on your self-esteem of the temperamental gap
between you and your mother.

Moving Past the Gaps

Once you have identified the gaps between yourself and your
mother, you are ready to take steps to get to know yourself better
and to free yourself from the barriers to your individual growth that
have resulted from these gaps.

Moving Past the Generation Gap

All mothers and daughters have the generation gap in their relationship, but it manifests in different ways depending on the mom
and the particular daughter. There are mothers who are stuck back
in their generation and haven't moved one iota away from that into
the current day. Then there are mothers who gladly gave up their
generation's standards and have moved into current-day values. But,
even this mother still has messages from her generation playing in
her head, and she can't give these up totally because that's where she
lived and she absorbed the ideals of her time. Here are the steps to
start moving beyond the generation gap so that you don't carry any
ideas from Mom's past life into your current one.

1. Think about what your mother's generation was concerned
with and how they lived their lives. What values did they hold? What
was important to them? How were women viewed? What was the
role of women? Read books about her generation and talk to her, if
you can, about what she observed and how she lived. What were the
expectations for her?

2. Once you have that information tucked into your belt, look
at today's landscape and see the differences between Mom's generation and yours. For example, perhaps the expectation back then was
to be married by a certain age, whereas today you have more choices
as to when or even if you marry.

3. Look to see what notions and expectations Mom has brought
forth from her past and deemed necessary in your life.

4. Separate out her past programming from what you know to
be right for you today.

5. Be constantly aware of what you are telling yourself about the
"shoulds" and "should-nots" in your life, and check them against
your list of what is right for you today.

Moving Past the Cultural Gap

You and your mom not only have a generation gap, but you may also have a cultural gap based on her living the ways of her culture and not fully adopting the attitudes and viewpoints of the culture she and you live in. This is not as easily dismissed as the generation gap, which is widely talked about and recognized. Instead, the cultural gap is much more invasive and your worth, in your mother's eyes, is often tied into whether you behave in the correct cultural manner. If you wish to distance yourself from this gap the following steps are necessary.

1. Find out why your mother's culture believes the way it does. What purpose did it serve to believe in that way? Was it a religious belief? Did it keep everyone safe in some way? Why hasn't her culture moved on and integrated with the current one?

2. Take a good look at how that culture differs from the one you are living in. There might be differences that are positive and others that are limiting and holding you back from fully experiencing life.

3. Once you have determined which views you like and want to keep from her culture and which you want to discard, make a list of those and start developing your own mix of cultures. You will have some of the old ways and some newer ways. It's a perspective uniquely your own, so value it as yours.

4. When your mother says something to you about life, pay attention to where this is coming from. She could be saying this simply because she didn't separate out for herself what was from the past with her own mother and what was current in her life. Don't take everything she says to heart, but examine it against your list and see if you want to accept her statement or not.

5. Be diligent in living your life based on your own values and modified standards. Know that Mom can believe any way she chooses—and so can you.

Moving Past the Temperament Gap

You may have determined that you and your mom possess the temperament gap, as each of you has a different way of looking at and interacting with life. Seeing this gap and recognizing what went on between the two of you is so freeing that now you want to move forward on your own. You wish to be absent from any judgments of you that were made from a different temperament than your own. The following steps are designed to loosen the hold this gap has had so that it is no longer a factor in your life.

1. You have taken the Temperament Momometer quiz and determined you and Mom were quite different people. Now, make a list of adjectives describing your mother and another one describing you.

2. Realize how your mom determined you were one way or another through her eyes. See why she believed the way she did. She saw you in a certain way, and you see how that happened, but now set that aside and start looking at yourself through your own eyes.

3. Take away any perceptions your mother had of you and start making a list of your own strengths and weaknesses. This will be an ever-changing list because as you mature your evaluation of your strengths and weaknesses changes. Something you thought was a weakness may turn into a strength and vice versa.

4. If your mother weren't your mother, would she be your friend? Your answer to this question speaks volumes about the compatibility of your temperaments. This will help you get over any thought that she or you were right or wrong. It may be just that you aren't that compatible. You can move on and not try to please her any longer.

5. When you have a good idea about who you are as opposed to who your mother said you were, go out and try on your new persona. You may trip every so often, but just pick yourself up, keep moving forward, and before you know it you will have changed the perception you have of you and become who you were meant to be.

Freedom from Mom

Factoring in all the gaps, the genes you were born with, messages that go back generations, coping mechanisms, individual fears and insecurities, and the perception you and your mother had of each other, you can see the mother-daughter relationship is similar to a hodgepodge of scents all mixed together. Separating the aromas out so you can determine your favorites for the next batch of perfume you are going to make takes some sleuthing, but once you train your nose to single out the different ingredients and subtract and add what works for you, you are on your way to self-satisfaction. It doesn't matter what Mom says or thinks is the right combination.

You've taken the blinders off and you are willing to confront reality—letting go of what you wanted your mom relationship to be or were taught by her to believe. Now, you're ready to take advantage of your newfound freedom and come into your own. Here are a few tips to get you on your way.

First, acknowledge your mother was not a deity in any sense of the word but just another person living on this earth. Take off the rose-colored glasses and do not make excuses for her behavior or thinking process. You don't have to condemn her entirely—unless that's truly warranted; just see her and the part of her web you have discovered in the bright light of reality. That's something that's easier said than done and takes rolling up your sleeves and doing some hard work.

It's like turning a snow globe upside down and letting the flakes settle once again. When the snow is floating around the scene is murky and not clearly visible, but when it clears you can see the details. In the mom-daughter connection the finer points will have changed shape and become clear once you have done your work, and the image now is one that is yours alone. You've taken the good parts of Mom and transformed the bad parts into a landscape all your own.

The second step toward freedom is introspection. Look clearly at where your mom has influenced your life, which this book will help you explore in the following chapters, being brutally honest about what behaviors of the mom gene you are carrying forth that you would rather not have—*thank you very much*. Once you have the broad picture of Mom's influence, or even suspect Mom is still in your life where you don't want her to be, oftentimes you will need a therapist to help you sort it all out, as you are too close to the fire to see the cause of this influence and its ramifications. It takes someone who is trained and objective to scope out the subtle ways you are reenacting your mom's life and to show you how she may have the last word in your choices and behavior.

The more you can see of this connection on your own the more information you take into therapy and the further along you are when you get there. You don't have to start at square one, not having a clue why your life isn't the way you imagined it to be, but can start at square three or square six on your path to greater awareness of your true role in life.

The third step is to start putting into practice this new way of being you exclusively, minus the mom gene. For example, if you need to learn to set correct boundaries for yourself because you weren't allowed to do that with Mom, you start with something small and let the momentum build until you are setting them in all areas.

For example, if you need to call the newspaper carrier and tell him not to throw your paper under the car every morning, and you hesitate because you don't want to hurt his feelings, go ahead and do it anyway. Your feelings are important also. If it hurts his feelings, so be it, you are now setting your boundaries, so watch out, world! Life really isn't going to change that much if you let your feelings be known about crawling under the car each day to retrieve the paper. And you might find it on the porch tomorrow!

When you start setting new boundaries in minor areas and seeing the results that boundary setting brings, expressing your needs begins to spread. Next thing you know you will be asking your mom to call first, please, and ask if this is a good time to visit rather than just announcing she is coming on such and such a day or time or showing up unannounced. Yes, your mother may want a relationship with you where she can just show up any old time, but perhaps you don't. Now you are beginning to be in charge of your own life, and you'll marvel at how easy it is once you get into the swing of doing it your way.

You are now aware of the mom gene, what it looks like, how it got there, and how it manifests. Now we are going to explore the different areas in which Mom has thrown her web over our lives—in love, sex, and aging. The next chapter is a look at love and how our mom plays a part in our choice of mates. Maybe you didn't think she was there, but indeed she is right in the middle of all our relationships.

3

Mom as Relationship Mentor

aura, twenty-three, had a new man in her life. Attractive in a wholesome, girl-next-door way, Laura lived at home with her stay-at-home mother and workaholic father. She and Kevin had met at an Italian deli; he accompanied her out to her car, where they started chatting and exchanged phone numbers. The short time they'd known each other since then had been spent perfectly. The dinner and conversation on their first date lasted for hours, and when they went bowling for their second rendezvous, they laughed the whole time.

Now Laura had been invited to a party given by Kevin's company. She'd spent hours getting ready, hoping to look just right when Kevin introduced her to his colleagues. She needed his approval, and the positive endorsement of his colleagues, just as she had always needed her mother's approval. What others thought about her was vastly important to her, as her mother had trained her well in this area. Getting ready, Laura's excitement had deteriorated to a huge case of the jitters. Her sense that he might be "the one" only intensified her nervousness.

Laura's mother seemed to be supportive. When Laura walked into the living room, her mother told her how nice she looked—words Laura badly needed to hear. Then, as Laura began confiding in her mom about how nervous she was and how much she really liked Kevin, the clincher came. Laura's mom said, "You look wonderful, of course . . . but do you have another pair of shoes you could wear?" Laura felt a ping in her stomach because she had on brand-new shoes that the saleslady had highly recommended for her new dress.

Laura then experienced a moment of clarity that had been brewing below the surface for some time—this is what her mother *always* did. Her mother acted supportive, but behind her comments Mom felt jealous of anyone Laura might admire. That was supposed to be reserved for Mom and Mom only. It wasn't that Laura's mom was trying to compete with her daughter in terms of appearance or looks—far from it. Her mother's real motivation was to keep Laura looking up to Mom as the expert forever.

By developing a serious interest in someone apart from her immediate family, Laura had unconsciously threatened a deep emotional need in her mother. Laura's mother was the kind of mom who intensely yearned to be needed by her children. Being a mother was her only important role in life, and she did everything she could think of to be that perfect mother.

She helped pick out Laura's clothes, she listened to all her thoughts and desires, and she directed her schoolwork and her professional career. There wasn't an area of Laura's life that Mom didn't try to play the starring role in, leading Laura to look to Mom to make sure she was living life correctly. The difficulty was that Mom's insecurities undermined Laura's self-confidence, leaving her open to basing her self-confidence on what someone else thought.

Moms' Roles in Their Daughters' Relationships

Consciously, most mothers try to do their best for their children. Yet for many reasons their efforts don't always fulfill their daughter's needs. Many moms fail to recognize that their own individual needs can interfere with what their children need and want. Laura's mom needed to be there for her "little girl" even when Laura was an adult who was starting to live her own life.

By questioning her choice of shoes, Mom was trying to hold on to her role in Laura's life and continue being the person who could approve or disapprove what Laura was wearing, saying, or doing. A man whom Laura had met on her own and with whom Laura was now starting to think about a future was presently threatening that dependency. Laura's mom felt her role in Laura's life was in jeopardy by her daughter shifting from needing her mom's approval to needing his.

Countless variables comprise the mother-daughter relationship, affecting the ways both daughters and mothers view their lives and the dynamics of the relationship between them. The combinations of these variables are endless, and can create difficulties when the daughter tries to become independent.

These can make the daughter's search for a healthy romantic relationship very challenging—as if another obstacle was needed on the path to a healthy romantic relationship. To determine how your mother influences your relationships, you first need to determine what kind of mothering style you have been brought up by and how such a style can affect your relationships.

Is Mom Affecting My Relationship?

- Do you feel like you have "settled for" a certain mate or type of relationship?
- Do you feel either superior or inferior to your mate?
- Do you have to *manage* your partner, or all hell breaks out?
- Does one of you play the silent treatment game?
- Is too much time spent away from the relationship by either one of you?
- Are your children your number one priority, even above your spouse?

- Are there way too many arguments?
- Do you think you could be denying excessive behaviors or addictions, either with yourself or your spouse, or at least be unwilling to confront them?
- Do you *only* go on separate vacations?
- Is there abuse of any kind going on?
- Do you have a general dissatisfaction with your relationship but can't seem to put your finger on what it is?
- Is there a lot of "come here"/"go away" going on?
- Is one of you excessively needy?
- Do you put up with undesirable behaviors just to keep the peace?
- Are there affairs going on now or in the past?
- Is one of you emotionally just not there?
- Is it more of a roommate relationship now than a romantic one?
- Is the reality of your relationship hard to look at for too long?

These are all indications that Mom is intruding on your relationship. Was your mother a needy, jealous mom like Laura's, or do you see her in one of the following mom styles?

No-Win Mother Relationship Styles

There are various mothering styles, and they each influence the relationship patterns daughters follow. Some mothers have healthy mom genes, but unfortunately, others don't. There are five categories of mothering styles that make it difficult for daughters to please their mothers, and this in turn influences the daughters' romantic relationship choices. These styles and their effects on daughters are described in detail later in this section.

1. **The Intrusive Center-Stage Mom.** Provokes a daughter's fear of losing herself in a relationship, or the daughter may seek to be controlled and/or approved of because of maternal smothering.
2. **The No-Show Mom.** The daughter harbors feelings of abandonment, which make her either needy in relationships or isolated from them.
3. **The Critic-at-Large Mom.** A daughter's learned low self-esteem due to her mother's constant critiques results in her choosing to become involved with someone either critical or more submissive than she is.
4. **The Helpless-Puppet Mom.** Results in involvement in relationships in which the daughter is either helpless herself or is a caretaker of others who are helpless.
5. **The Drama-Queen Mom.** The daughter latches onto partners too quickly and/or chooses men who are emotionally unavailable.

If your mom fits one of the aforementioned mothering types, oftentimes your romantic relationships as an adult aren't as fulfilling as they could be. As a result of these, you can fall into one of two traps. You can either choose to adopt your mom's style as your own, thus enabling the mom gene to continue in your life and turning out to be just like your mom, or you can choose to carry out your relationships in a totally opposite manner, which still ties you into your mom's messages, albeit more subtly. Whether you do the same or you do the opposite, it's all the same trap because either way, your mom is the sole influence on how you experience your relationships.

Let's examine more closely the mothering styles that influence daughters' ideas and behaviors in romantic relationships, keeping in mind which trap your relationship gene is falling into.

The Intrusive Center-Stage Mom

This type of mother lives her life through her daughter and strives mightily to make everything wonderful for her. But the real goal is to look like the most perfect mother in existence and be given the Mother-of-the-Year award. She pours her life into her daughter and needs to have that distinction noticed by not only her daughter, but by the rest of her family and friends. She's given up her own life to achieve this crowning glory, and woe unto the daughter who doesn't recognize and appreciate her mother's efforts.

To help her efforts to be fully realized, this kind of mother has chosen a mate who allows her to devote her life to her daughter. Intrusive Mom doesn't want a husband who is an equal partner or a man who needs to be in charge of the family. Mom has total authority in this home, and the husband she's chosen has little self-confidence and no desire to stand up to her. In fact, he has no need to be an active parent in his child's life. Mom has chosen the opposite of an equal partner.

This husband could possibly take the form of some type of "-holic"—alcoholic, workaholic, sportsaholic, or sexaholic. Spending more energy doing anything other than being an active husband and/or father puts him in this category. He escapes into these behaviors and ignores what is going on around him. When his wife complains about him and pushes him away—voila!—she very conveniently has center stage. And what a martyr she is, because she has to put up with him. How very clever. She's now on the list for two prestigious awards, "Best Mother" and the "Oh, Look What I've Had to Put Up With" award.

If she didn't marry a "-holic" of some sort, the Intrusive Center-Stage Mom may have married a man who is passive, someone with whom she doesn't have to compete, or someone who is emotionally unresponsive. He plays the role of the emotionally absent father and abdicates his power and authority to the person who intended to have it all along—his wife.

This relationship actually works for these two parents, because both of their roles in life are exactly what they want them to be. There may be fighting and arguing and lots of tension in the marriage, or their relationship could be so superficial that one wonders how they ever got together in the first place, but this is exactly what these parents need and want, strange as this may seem to the uninitiated observer.

Besides intrusive, these mothers are called Center-Stage Moms because the entertainment field is rife with them. Teri Shields, Brooke Shields's mother, was famous for trying to control her daughter's career, and if you get involved with theater, dance, music, or acting where children are involved, you will see these mothers trying to assert power over their daughter's life in all areas.

CHRISTINE

Christine was a very gifted young girl; she could sing, dance, and act. Her mother was there for all classes and performances. Her father, supposedly too busy with work, would only attend a performance or two, arriving just at starting time and leaving as soon as it was over. Christine's mother made sure her daughter was a success in all areas, telling her what and what not to eat, choosing all her clothes, driving her to after-school activities, and even doing some of her homework so Christine could concentrate more completely on her craft.

Her mother even went so far as to volunteer at each performance to make sure Christine did everything correctly. This way, she would also know her daughter's boyfriends and could weed out the ones she disapproved of.

Christine's mother's motive was to involve herself in every aspect of her daughter's life because Christine was her life. If a boy happened to show any interest in Christine, her mother would accidentally misplace phone messages from him and do her darnedest to ensure the young couple had no time alone, effectively discouraging the young man and so keeping her place as number one in her daughter's life.

When Christine graduated from high school, she could hardly wait to move out of state and away from her mother's influence. She attended a performing arts college across the country and then halfheartedly worked at trying to make it on Broadway.

Today Christine's still not sure if acting was ever her driving interest or if her mother has simply pushed too hard and destroyed any joy Christine might have found from her talents. Christine waits tables now and has dated some young men, but she is so afraid of being smothered again in any fashion that she can't maintain a relationship for long. As she puts it, "I couldn't figure out why I always found something wrong with the men I dated until I saw a therapist who helped me understand I had a very strong mother who took control of my life. The last thing I want [in a relationship] is another Mom. If I have to forgo a relationship [right now] to have my freedom, so be it. Hopefully, I won't feel this way forever. Someday I want children of my own, but I'll do motherhood differently than my own mother did."

A daughter with this type of mother will approach relationships in one of two ways. She will do what Christine did and avoid control—or even the feeling of being controlled—at all costs. Or she will believe that unless she is controlled she won't know how else to live, so she will look for a mate who can make decisions and to whom she can take a backseat. If this was the mothering style you grew up with, which side do you find yourself closest to? You might not fall completely into one camp, but you will lean more to one side than the other. Decide what it is for you, and we will next discuss how to reprogram this gene.

WHAT TO DO. Having an Intrusive Center-Stage Mom requires you to look for specific needs that didn't get filled as you were growing up. This allows you to see how that loss has affected your adult life and relationships. Once you identify the particular voids in your life you can start the journey in working on them to allow yourself to have better and happier relationships.

With this type of mother, oftentimes you need to have others recognize and respect you and your feelings, since Mom didn't give them a glance. You may choose a mate you can control so as not to have to trust another with your emotions and insecurities. You may feel that it's safer to not have anyone know about your void, so you cover it up by being in the power position. You think if you don't expose your void you can't get hurt again, but still the void remains.

You have to first accept that other people can't fill this void because it stems from so long ago. Needs or voids from the past can't be met by anyone today because they are not present-day needs. You are the only one who can fill that hole. You have to learn to listen to, accept, and respect your own thoughts and feelings. If you feel a certain way, accept that is how you feel and that it's not right or wrong. Others don't have to feel the same way, but it's okay for you to.

The more you accept your feelings, the more connected you will be with yourself, and slowly your void will be filled. Then you won't have to control anyone or anything to hide what's really inside of you. You will become comfortable with yourself and others will become comfortable with you. It's a win-win situation.

On the other side of the coin, if you have chosen the path of needing someone to lead your life, acknowledge that, however painful the realization may be. This flip side is also caused by not having access to your self-worth, or any knowledge of yourself, as

Mom didn't teach you how to be you and how to love and treasure the person you are. She was too busy getting her own needs met, but it's your turn now.

If you see that you continually get into relationships in which you need to be led, first make the decision to learn who you are separate and apart from anyone else. This doesn't mean you have to run off to a mountaintop in India and live there for years, but it does require you to start asserting yourself to learn who you are. First start in little areas and work up to larger ones. If you want to eat whole-wheat bread while everyone else in your family wants white, for example, go down to the store and buy yourself some heavy-duty brown bread.

You don't have to rock the whole boat, but you can do what is good for you regardless of what someone else says or wants as long as what you do doesn't infringe on others. Practicing assertiveness with the smallest details has a compound effect, and when you have enough experiences with the small matters you will be able to go on to make more important decisions. You will become a part of the whole relationship, not just a follower in it.

The No-Show Mom

It takes a lot of effort and practice to fulfill a child's needs so that the child grows into a responsible, healthy, and emotionally secure adult. Moms who do not fulfill their child's emotional needs are called No-Show Moms. The body is there, but the heart is missing. Many of these No-Show Moms are obvious, such as the alcoholic, the mentally ill, the physically or sexually abusive mom, or the mom who died while her daughter was young.

Other No-Show Moms aren't so obvious. These are the mothers who go through the motions of the mother role but have little or no emotional connection to their children. For this type of mother, raising her children is simply a duty, and she fulfills this duty only because it's the right thing to do. Mom may put the job of babysitting younger siblings on her daughter's shoulders, as she may be busy with a career or enjoying an active social life, or she may be preoccupied with her husband, putting him first over her daughter. Maybe Mom is trying to be Volunteer of the Year at the local hospital, or she may have so many children to raise that the children come in second to the mundane tasks of a large family.

She may understand on some level that she isn't connected with her children. She may even take it a step further and make it the child's fault that the bond isn't there. Then the child gets the message there is something wrong with her, leaving a gaping hole in the child's quest for adulthood.

NAOMI

A No-Show Mom raised Naomi and her brother. It all started after Naomi's mom found out her fun-loving, life-of-the-party husband had had an affair, resulting in another woman's pregnancy.

Her heart broken, Naomi's mother split from her husband, vowing never to fall in love again. She chose as her second husband a boring yet stable man—from whom she kept a safe emotional distance. When her new husband moved the family to the Midwest to pursue his dream of being a farmer, Naomi's mother felt stuck and trapped. She felt she couldn't leave and strike out on her own because of the financial difficulties she'd encounter raising two young children.

At age five, little Naomi had to deal with a new dad, a new location, a new life . . . and a desperately unhappy mother. When twin girls were born, Naomi saw her stepfather lavish all his attention on his biological children, while she never saw or even heard from her own biological father.

As Naomi grew up, her depressed mother failed to lavish much affection on her, only sending her daughter messages that reflected her own desire for independence and her needs for emotional and mental stimulation. She told Naomi over and over how important it was to have an education and to avoid having babies at a young age, as she had done, because this would curtail Naomi's freedom.

Partly because of the lack of an emotional connection with her mother and partly to prove her mother wrong, Naomi became pregnant at fifteen. When her mother informed her she was to raise the child on her own, Naomi did the only thing she knew to do: she married the father of her soon-to-be-born daughter.

The marriage had no chance of survival: her husband, a verbally abusive drug addict, soon began to physically abuse Naomi and their daughter. Naomi walked out, only to return a short time later when her husband went into rehab. Her main motivation to make the marriage work was to prove her mother wrong about life, children, and relationships. When it became clear to Naomi that the rehab hadn't worked and her husband hadn't changed, she left and began searching for a man who was better relationship material. Yet Naomi soon found and married another man with as many problems as the first.

Naomi chooses dysfunctional men who need her help, thereby ensuring she will be loved for her generous, giving spirit and that she won't be abandoned. Because she does not have a loving dad present, she tries to prove to all men she is a good person. She wants to prove her mother wrong in her assessment that a woman loses all freedom of choice once she has children. If she can prove her mother wrong, that would prove her mother's assessment of her was wrong also.

Unfortunately, Naomi has not yet been able to overcome the damage done to her self-esteem by her mother and later by Naomi's husbands, and when Naomi and her second husband decided to move to Hawaii, Naomi left her daughter with the child's biological father, repeating her own mother's behavior even though she had experienced firsthand what it felt like to be the child of a No-Show Mom. Naomi has effectively become her mother.

Daughters of the No-Show Mom often choose a mate who allows them to be in the superior position in one form or another. As in Naomi's case, this could take the form of the wife as the rescuer who is going to start her husband on the road to a happier life, thus ensuring that he will be so indebted he will never leave her. For instance, maybe he has a big fault either in appearance, financial position, or emotional accessibility and is so grateful to her for being in his life that he buys her affection or stays in the little boy role so that he gives her life meaning and value by allowing her to try to fix him.

If he has financial security and gives to her monetarily she's being taken care of in that area while she is still in charge in another area. It looks as if both are getting their needs met, but outsiders often sense a lack of emotional closeness between the couple. Their relationship may always be that way . . . and it may not. Many couples go for many years, sometimes a lifetime, with this type of disconnected relationship working for them, but for others, it's doomed to fail once one or both of them realize they have greater needs that must be met for them to be fulfilled.

WHAT TO DO. When unmet needs prevail and overcome logic, you may unwittingly fall back on what was familiar during your growing-up years. The strength and magnitude of your needs cause you to react emotionally rather than intellectually. You may know something intellectually but be unable to access this information when the emotional side comes into play, and since the emotional side governs your behavior, you may often act in ways that are a result of past conditioning. Major change of the mom gene takes true diligence, so you may need an impartial observer to help you see when you've fallen into an old pattern of behavior or exhibit your mother's pattern. Understanding this conditioning and pattern of behavior with your intellectual mind is only the first step, albeit an important one, toward behavioral change.

Being a daughter of a No-Show Mom usually results in wanting to belong to someone, as abandonment issues loom large for this daughter. If you feel like you just have to be with a mate, and you go from relationship to relationship with nary a breath in between, or you hang on to a relationship that is going nowhere, stop and ask yourself if you had a No-Show Mom. She's sure to be lurking there somewhere, and once you decide you had this mom you can start to heal the wound she left you with.

On the other side of the coin, if you are keeping relationships at arm's length because of insecurities and think, "If I don't have it I can't lose it," you are also manifesting a No-Show Mom gene. Either compromising yourself to gain security or making sure some man isn't going to ever leave you by not getting involved in the first place is a high price to pay, and you might want to reconsider your options after learning what legacy Mom left you with.

The result of being a daughter of this mom means you were expected to know how to live life without being given any kind of script at all. You had no one to guide you as to how to be a stand-on-your-own woman. If this is true for you, start by doing whatever it takes to build up your sense of worth. It might be going back to school for a degree, working with children, learning how to cook or swim or dance, or learning about the stock market.

Whatever experiences you decide to invest in, get out on your own and experience the world to see what it has to offer you. Some experiences will resonate, while others won't. A healthy mom offers her daughter this freedom to find herself, and now you can do it for yourself. Once you have succeeded in knowing your likes and dis-likes, your strengths and weaknesses, you can walk into a relationship secure enough that you won't be afraid to be abandoned because you will still have yourself.

If you are in a relationship currently, that is fine, as long as your self isn't lost in the midst of it. If you find all of you really isn't there, then "Know thyself and don't let go of you" is a good motto for you and one you might want to paste on your bathroom mirror to look at and work toward on your quest for selfdom.

The Critic-at-Large Mom

No matter how you try to please her, there is always something you could have done better or smarter, or maybe you shouldn't have done it at all. Meet the Critic-at-Large Mom. She jots down every mistake you have ever made and will have them made into a movie for everyone to see.

The hypercritical mother meets her need to be in charge by mak-ing her children believe she has all the right answers when she really isn't the expert at all. It's important to note, since this mom really doesn't know who her daughter is or what she is capable of, she isn't criticizing her daughter as a person. The behavior is simply a ploy to keep the focus away from Mom because inside she believes she is unworthy.

The Critic-at-Large Mom really doesn't have the capability to look at another person, her daughter or anyone else, with a clear, unbiased vision. With every "I told you so" and "Why are you doing it that way?" a vicious cycle begins. The more the mother feels unworthy and tries to exhibit an air of knowledge and authority through offering criticism, the more her daughter's self-esteem is chipped away and she begins to question every ounce of her being.

At the core of both mother and daughter is the feeling of being unworthy. The mother feels undeserving and passes that same sentiment to her daughter. Unworthiness affects daughters who grew up under this mom gene and buries the ability to get close to another and, gulp—to trust. Now we have two women in the family who are searching for love but never finding true intimacy because the need to please others, which is the manifestation of the fear of abandonment, keeps getting in the way. Critical mothers and their daughters hide a vulnerability that is buried deep inside of them. Their defenses are impenetrable; the little girl inside doesn't want to be hurt ever again.

ROBIN

As a child, Robin was an excellent student. She got good grades, was well behaved at home, and had a few close friends—but still her mother found ways to be critical. The message was always, "Do what I tell you to do." Whatever Robin did was never good enough, and she got the message that even her best wasn't worthy enough.

Robin married, divorced, and then met Bill, an extremely good-looking man with a steady job. Bill had been raised in a very strict religious family where everyone was made to toe a very narrow line, defined by his parents. He always had someone to tell him right from wrong and was never allowed to develop his own character traits.

Throughout their relationship Robin would complain when Bill gained a few pounds or missed a workout. She told him he never selected the right cheese at the store, that he never chose the right car or the right song on the radio. She thought he should be more successful in his professional life and never let him forget that. At one of their many parties and in front of their guests, she berated him for not taking pictures at a certain time. Then she told him the pictures weren't of the right people.

In a way, Bill was the perfect man for Robin: he believed there wasn't much he could do correctly, while Robin used her mom gene to exhibit authority through criticism. Bill needed Robin's guidance through life, and most of the time he was willing to put up with her criticisms to obtain the leadership she provided.

Robin and Bill have married and divorced twice now. Robin is at odds not only with her family but also with his. They both know this isn't the best relationship for them, but when they pull apart, abandonment issues surface and they run as fast as they can back to each other.

Robin manifested this mom gene by being exactly like her mother and finding someone who allowed her to criticize him, therefore keeping him indebted to her just as her mother did to her. It starts the cycle all over again, but this daughter can't expose herself to more abandonment. She's been there and done that and isn't going back for more, so she hides her fears of being found unlovable under her criticism of others.

JANE

In contrast to Robin, Jane was a meek and docile thirty-five-year-old woman who relied on everyone in her circle of friends and family to help her live her life. She was extremely dependent on her mate, asking him what clothes she should buy, where their children should go to school, and how long she could stay out in the evening without him. As much as it seemed to Jane that she had a supportive husband and a secure life, she could not shake off her feelings of depression.

Jane entered therapy and realized that her own mother had been raised by a critical mother, and thus became critical of

Jane. As Jane was growing up, her mother had asked why the As on her report card were not A-plusses. Jane's mother didn't know a different way to relate to her daughter and her accomplishments because she had never been exposed to other options. By the time Jane was an adult she had developed such an inferiority complex she was unable to make an independent decision.

Depression is often the feeling of anger turned inward, and Jane began to see how her mother's constant criticism contributed to her feelings of anger, hurt, and consequently depression as she was growing up. Now she had chosen a mate who also made her feel she was not good enough, thus enabling her feelings of inferiority and self-doubt.

As Jane began to see the effects of being raised by a hypercritical mom and moved toward change, her husband, feeling threatened, insisted she stop therapy. For the time being, Jane has complied.

The Critic-at-Large Mom's tyranny over her daughter starts in childhood and continues through the adult daughter's life. For this daughter, the ability to move away emotionally from her mother's demeaning ways will be a long battle because she has grown so dependent on someone else telling her when she is right or wrong that she has no sense of self. Growth doesn't come easily because her mother's criticisms have infiltrated both her conscious and subconscious mind, affecting her ability to function as a self-assured person both in and out of relationships. Ruthless self-criticism and self-doubt rear their ugly heads in any endeavor she undertakes.

Because this daughter hungered for her mom's approval, which never came in any meaningful way, she may constantly look to the people in her life for reassurance. Always needing someone else's approval but never having the confidence to believe it or fully accept it leaves this daughter with the same nagging self-doubt. It's like playing the childhood game Mother May I? over and over again all through her life, always waiting for permission to act.

Some daughters of critical moms will enjoy success in their professional lives, but in their personal lives, this take-charge attitude evaporates. When asked by her husband where they should go on vacation, she will reply, "Where do you want to go?" She doesn't dare make a decision herself, for fear of not getting the answer correct. Her greatest fear is opening herself up to criticism. Remember, the daughter of the Critic-at-Large Mom has been raised to accede to another person's opinions and to value those opinions at the expense of her own. She carries this dynamic into her adult relationships.

WHAT TO DO. To eradicate the critical mom gene in your life and to ensure it's not passed on to future generations, daughters must first identify the family trait and then be able to recognize that they have taken up that very same behavior themselves.

It could be that you are the one criticizing your mate, or you could be with someone who criticizes you, but, either way, the disapproval shows up, and your Critic-at-Large Mom is the one who taught you this ploy. You must disregard this manner of relating so that you can have healthy relationships that meet your needs of being loved and loving.

One way to circumvent the old messages is to find where your boundaries are and verbalize them to others. This constitutes thinking about what works for you and what doesn't, what you want in your life and what you don't want, and then being willing to tell others in your life how you feel no matter if that's what they want or not.

If you don't want to be called after 9:00 P.M. you must verbalize that boundary to those who do call you later. If you don't want to be patted on the rear end every time your honey gets close, but you enjoy a kiss hello and good-bye, you need to tell him. If family members drop in any old time they choose and that isn't your style, your job is to tell them in a nice but firm way. Boundaries are personal to each individual, so find what yours are and start expressing them. No matter what others think or say and if they criticize loudly or just give you a look that says, "You're all wrong," remember this is your life to live as you choose without worrying about another person's opinion of you.

Each time you are able to express your true feelings, reward yourself with something that has meaning to you because you've started erasing the critical mom gene in your life. Maybe it's flowers, new shoes, a luxurious bath, or a ride on a Ferris wheel. Whatever the reward, the goal is to determine the magnitude of what you've accomplished and honor yourself accordingly. It's not always easy to think of yourself first, but that is exactly what you must do to be an equal part of any friendship or relationship. That way you are always present as yourself and not just a puppet to everyone else, trying to please them so they don't critique and criticize you.

Not relying on others' judgment of you takes strength, and each time you do this it's big news, as you are saying, "Hey, I'm also a person here with needs, wants, and desires, and they are appropriate." Others may wonder what happened to you, but you know you have just parented yourself and grown up.

The Helpless-Puppet Mom

The daughter of the Helpless–Puppet Mom never gets to be a child in the true sense of the word. She can't depend on her mother for nurturing and guidance through her own anxieties or insecurities because she has to fill that need in her incredibly anxious and insecure mother. This mother gets the "vapors" and takes to her bed, literally or figuratively, leaving the daughter to cope on her own.

The Helpless-Puppet Mom's desire is to be as closely linked to her children as possible. As adults, some daughters gravitate toward their mother's idea of closeness, sometimes living with their mother or staying in the same town to be nearby. Other daughters of this mother type put as much distance as they can between themselves and their mother, perhaps choosing a location in the other side of the world to live. Which route a daughter chooses indicates the type of love relationships that person gravitates to and is most comfortable in.

KIM

Kim took care of everyone in her life—her husband, her children, her parents, her friends, and anyone else who crossed her path. She felt that being a caretaker of others was her God-given role in life, and she was determined to do the job perfectly. It was what her mother had expected of her as a child. Kim was the one who went to the store on her bike when Mom ran out of milk, and she cooked dinner when Mom decided, for whatever reason, she wasn't able to. Kim was expected to get herself up and ready for school from the time she was five. She would bring water and handpicked flowers to her mom and sit with her when Mom was having a bad day, setting aside her own playtime to help Mom.

Kim learned to put her own needs aside in the interest of others. But instead of the people in her adult life seeing her as their rescuer, whom they were indebted to for her kindness and unswerving devotion, they treated her as their servant. She played this role as she drove her children to their many activities; she was Girl Scout leader, soccer mom, chief cook and bottle washer, and family chauffeur. She did her husband's ironing and supported him in his career, which took him out of town on business trips, leaving her to operate as a single parent. When he was home, her husband corrected her behavior and left her notes listing what she had done wrong around the house. In addition, he insisted that she work outside the home to help support the family.

Over time, Kim developed stress-related health problems; her doctor advised her to slow down, telling her she couldn't be all things to all people, no matter how hard she tried. This foreign concept stunned Kim. Of course she had to serve everyone . . . didn't she?

Kim had carried forward the role her mother assigned to her—caretaker of all. She was still acting out the Helpless-Puppet Mom scenario of her childhood, ignoring her own needs and wishes.

Whether you act out the same role your mother did or take the opposing role, you are still playing out your mother's relationship script. In this case, you either become a helpless puppet yourself, grooming your children to fill your neediness, or you try to fill other people's needs as you did with your mother. Having this type of mother guarantees you were never able to express your emotions around her. She was much too fragile to handle them—fainting couches suit this mother wonderfully.

JANET

When Janet, tall and beautiful, graduated from high school, she went away to college and never looked back. Her move half a continent away allowed her to escape the nursemaid role her mother expected of her. The cries of, "You never come to see me" and "Don't you love me?" no longer moved Janet. As an adult she was much too independent by temperament to get lost in her mother's so-called frailties.

Nevertheless, Janet has paid a high price for being raised by this mother. Relationships of any kind are scary for her. Her biggest fear is that the other person would try to swallow her up just as her mother had done. She has dated many men but always finds something wrong with them. Janet, now fifty-five and a real estate broker, remains relationship-free, even though she yearns on some level for someone to love and craves love in return. Her anger over her mother's treatment keeps a distance between her and any potential mate because Janet's mom gene taught her that.

Janet has now entered therapy and her past assumption that relationships are not to be trusted because they devalue independence is losing its hold on her life. Janet is now actively looking for a relationship in which she can create a balance with a partner that would allow her the independence she needs and at the same time afford her the emotional connection she wants.

The daughter of a Helpless-Puppet Mom has a difficult time expressing her emotions, so they build up over time and turn into unresolved anger, which can show itself in a myriad of ways. She might be over- or underweight, experience headaches or other physical problems, or not care about her appearance, or she can bury herself with work, friends, or children. These can all be symptoms of resentments from long ago, and if you had this type of mother you will need to flush them out so you can move on to become a happier, more content person.

In relationships, unresolved anger can come out either directly at a partner or through passive-aggressive behavior, which often causes your mate to express the anger you can't. This doesn't speak well for a relationship. The rough spots never get resolved because the underlying causes are never ferreted out and addressed. The anger keeps building with no safe way to release it.

WHAT TO DO. Every child deserves to be a child, playing and socializing with other children and growing up, age by age and step-by-step, at her own pace. Since the Helpless-Puppet Mom is unable to provide a safe shelter in the world for her daughter, her daughter is required to grow up much too fast. This damages her ability to function in relationships that are healthy for her as an adult as she lacks the capability to be assertive or to believe her needs are important in a relationship. She gives away too much of herself to others and thus stays lost to the real person she is. In other cases she may stay away from relationships because she's too focused on her own needs and doesn't want anyone to dictate any part of her life.

If you find this was the mothering style you were exposed to, start believing that your needs are worthwhile, just as the other person's needs are equally important. To do this you may have to listen to the little girl inside of you that didn't get a chance to be playful because she never got her time in the sun. Talk to her and ask her what she wants to do and how she feels.

She will answer you, and it might be surprising what she comes up with. If she wants to go to the park and swing, take her. If she wants to splash in rain puddles, let her. Maybe she would love an ice cream cone with sprinkles. This is her time to be a little girl and do things she missed out on earlier. If you indulge her she can learn to grow up to be an adult—the adult who is you.

If you discover you either subjugate yourself in a relationship or you don't trust relationships and have none, or only very superficial ones, look for the anger you are harboring. Knowing the anger is there, and being determined to see how it's manifesting in your life, leads you to the next step of releasing the anger within.

Achieving this goal may take some time in therapy to learn healthy ways of releasing anger, or you might try keeping a journal about your feelings and learn other ways to express yourself rather than turning your anger inward. You just might find you are a very worthwhile person whom you adore underneath it all. Positive affirmations are another avenue to recognize your worth. Affirmations are statements you repeat many times to yourself that assist your conscious mind in focusing on what you want to achieve or create in your life. They counter negative self-beliefs and can lead your subconscious mind into creating the situation you desire. It's like *The Little Engine That Could* who starts out saying, "I think I can, I think I can" and changes it to "I know I can, I know I can" and makes it to the top of the mountain. He was using a positive affirmation to change his outcome and you can, too. Whatever works for you is the right way, and you are the only one who should decide your path.

The Drama-Queen Mom

This mother is determined to have the world revolve around her. She's the star of her own soap opera, and those within her scope of influence, including her husband and her children, are all relegated to bit parts. She will do just about anything to ensure she remains the diva of her family by overdramatizing every small and large event of her life to make sure her family's life is centered on her.

The breaking of a fingernail is a major catastrophe—God forbid! How can she possibly go to the gym with a broken nail? Her daughter is involved in a minor car accident, and Mom carries on like it's the end of the world. Whether it's a minor occurrence, which most of them are, or a major life event, all receive the same dramatic treatment. A healthy reaction to anything in life is not within her scope of desire or ability.

If it takes screaming, fighting, rage, physical abuse, or degrading those closest to her, she's up for the challenge. No one is going to rain on her parade. For a husband she chooses a man who allows himself to be her victim, and she starts her children young in learning their bit parts in the play she has cleverly crafted. She's the star and won't let anyone forget it, especially her daughter, who simply by being female threatens to take her place or show her up. There can only be one leading light in her family . . . and the Drama-Queen Mom makes sure it is she.

She can be a bully who metes out corporal punishment as she sees fit. She's a master of verbal abuse, either subtle or full-blown, having learned the ins and outs of psychological damage from her parents. Everyone else's actions are criticized, belittled, and shamed. Any accomplishment her daughter enjoys only brings down this mother's wrath even harder to guarantee Mom is still the queen bee. Think of *Mommie Dearest* and you get the picture. If there is closeness between her daughter and her husband, watch out, as jealousy will raise its ugly head. She doesn't want to play second fiddle to anyone in her family, and that includes her husband. He's supposed to be there in name only, not to take attention away from her.

This mother needs the star position with her family because she has been running scared all of her life. She has been insecure since she was a little girl and has learned to cover up her shortcomings with dramas and attention-demanding behavior, subtle or otherwise. She is living constantly with the panic that she might be discovered as a fraud, so she learned long ago how to control that fear of exposure through histrionics. By constantly terrorizing others or inventing crises this mother keeps the attention on the outside, never having to look anywhere else for the cause of her troubles.

SARAH

Sarah, the twenty-three-year-old daughter of a Drama-Queen Mom, is petite, attractive, and intelligent. She is finishing her master's degree in social work and plans to specialize in the treatment of abused children. She knows the damage done to these children . . . because she grew up being abused, verbally and physically, by her mother. Her mother terrorized her constantly, telling Sarah she was no good and hitting her for unknown transgressions. When her mother was especially angry she would yell at Sarah saying she wished she had never given birth to a daughter like her.

Daughters of such dysfunctional mothers seek someone they can go to for comfort and support, not knowing what exactly they are supposed to be looking for in a long-term relationship. This need for safety has caused Sarah to seek out relationships she can get involved in fairly quickly, oftentimes moving way too fast.

Her every thought is about her current mate, and she graces his doorstep carrying chicken soup and fresh-squeezed orange juice at the sign of the slightest sniffle even if she has just known him for a couple of weeks. She is hoping for and craving the attention and love from him she didn't receive as a child from Mom. If these men have given her even a little bit of attention and thanks, she obsesses about them long after the breakup. Sarah was so underprovided for in learning to have any self-worth at all that she hangs on for dear life to anyone who even gives her the slightest sense of value, whether that person is still in the picture or not.

Sarah is still young, and she is hoping that she will learn, in time, to cast off her mom issue of expecting much less from a relationship than what she is really worth. She wants a healthy relationship, and she wants to feel good about herself whether she's in one or not. Only after removing the mom gene residue can she begin the journey to find her real self.

Other Drama-Queen Moms are subtler in their approach than Sarah's mother was. They may not be as easy to spot as the more overt types, but they cause just as much damage to their daughters. They are the matriarchs of their families, and if you look closely you can see that they rule in a backhanded way. They maintain control at all costs, emphasizing that all that matters is themselves and their narcissistic needs without a second glance at anyone else's requirements in life. That is how these drama queens manifest their insecurities—"Look, over here, it's all about me"—they demand that you forget who you are and focus on them.

ASHLEY

Ashley was in her forties and thought she had finally gotten it right this time. Through a chance meeting at her brother's house, she met Tom, who was visiting from England. He had been recently widowed, and almost immediately, he and Ashley felt a connection. When they parted they exchanged e-mails and eventually met up in New York, where they spent a glorious week getting to know each other better. More vacations were planned and spent together, and when Tom proposed marriage Ashley joyously accepted.

However, during a visit to St. Tropez before their plans were complete, Tom confessed to Ashley that he was having a hard time thinking about leaving his family and friends in England to live with Ashley in California. Ashley knew this was serious because his demeanor had changed toward her. Where he had previously been loving and attentive to her, he now was distant and cool. Tom finally admitted that he couldn't make the move, and Ashley came home in tears. Her dream of finding that special person to share a life with seemed to be falling apart.

In distress Ashley turned to her mother for support and described what had happened with her marriage plans. But Ashley's mom soon turned the subject onto herself and began carrying on about her broken dishwasher and then hung up.

Ashley needed sensitivity, time, and understanding from her mother, but her mother, wrapped up in her own needs as usual, brushed off Ashley's pain and turned the attention back to her own world. Her mother wanted the play to revolve around herself, and to heck with anyone else's desires or needs. After the conversation with her mother Ashley felt more fragile and strung out than ever.

It's not surprising that many daughters of the Drama-Queen Mom pick men who are not there for them emotionally in the long run. The Drama Queen makes sure the focus is on her so that her daughter learns at an early age to disregard her own needs. This attitude transfers to the daughter's adult relationships with men. When she looks for a mate, she attracts self-serving men, the exact opposite of the kind of man she needs. She learned the program her mother taught, and while she may not like it, she will keep going back for more of the same, continuing the pattern of denying her own needs in a relationship.

WHAT TO DO. You may have had the loud, in-your-face Drama-Queen Mom, and you may have had the subtler one with whom the drama was quieter and the queen element shouted the loudest, but whichever one you were blessed with means there is a part of you that doesn't feel important and special.

Whether you choose unavailable, self-centered men who think it's all about them—just like Mom—or you quickly latch onto and have a hard time letting go of a partner who you thought cared about you—like Mom never did—breaking the mom spell over your life takes a willingness to accept that as a child you didn't get seen or taken into consideration. Maybe Mom didn't even like you because she felt threatened simply because you were who she wasn't.

Now you have to learn to be special in your own eyes, and you must do whatever it takes to achieve that distinction within yourself. If you had dreams in childhood that didn't get realized, this is a good time to investigate that area and see where it leads you. Take your time to check out all the aspects of your goal. If it is to be in a partnership don't move too quickly deciding a man is the one and only before you know him completely. Remember, you can't just take some parts of a person and ignore the rest. It's all one package, and that takes time to investigate and experience. Slow down and let yourself take the relationship step-by-step rather than latching on to him at the first fluttering of your heart. Don't give up on your other dreams, but pursue them also as they are just as important.

Dormant dreams that were never given free rein offer a glimpse into a part of you that wasn't allowed to come to fruition. By pursuing those dreams and goals now you will reconnect with that inner child and begin to feel special to yourself. Put enough dreams together and you will find that self-worth is yours for the taking.

Learning to put a high value on yourself is a must for the daughter of a Drama-Queen Mom. There is always a feeling of not being good enough and also a worry that if someone sees inside of you he or she will discover all of those parts that don't measure up. Know that this is simply the message your mom gave you, and it isn't true in the slightest sense.

Give yourself compliments all the time for the smallest wins in your life to the largest. If you let a driver in your busy lane, know that you have just performed an act of kindness. When you smile at someone walking down the street and that person smiles back, you have just earned yourself another pat on the back. If you will just recognize and acknowledge the many positive things you do you will begin your course in building self-esteem—remembering self-esteem is the reputation *you* have of you. You can continue to build on this and realize the person you really are out of Mom's web.

Outwit the Mom Gene

Now that you understand the various mothering styles that affect relationships, you can see clearly the mom gene that threatens your relationships. Unearthing the mom gene as it works in relationships isn't always easy, and it's not always fun, but it is imperative if you want a different relationship style in your life. Whether you're already connected in a relationship or are single, you can make changes within yourself, thereby assuring a different and better bond with another person.

Only by recognizing and outwitting the mom gene can you forge a new pathway to better and healthier relationships. If you want to live life differently, *what do you have to lose by changing your perception of yourself?* You have little to lose and much to gain.

So step back for a moment and look at your life as if through someone else's eyes. Tell yourself or write in a journal your life story, beginning with the relationship you had with your mother through all of your other relationships to where you are now. See what links, or similarities, you find as the common thread that connects your mother-daughter relationship to all other relationships in your life. Everyone has different threads from Mom to others, and the following questions will get you started thinking about where and how to find these connections.

For example, if you find that you attract needy people, look to see if your mom was needy and you were the caretaker. Or perhaps your mom was totally in charge, so you choose someone who isn't because you didn't like that about her. In either case the thread goes from Mom to others in your life.

You might find the thread starting with Mom. If you recognize that Mom was uptight and rigid about money, you may see you choose mates who are the same either with money or ideas. Or you may go the opposite way and find someone who is careless in financial and personal matters. If you find a pattern with people in your adult life, trace it back to Mom, and conversely when you identify a trait of Mom's, trace that forward and see what you have done with it. It's enlightening when you get the hang of it, so start with these questions and see where they lead you.

- **Which types of people are repeatedly in your life?** Are they givers, takers, pessimists, or domineering individuals?

- **What is the emotional availability of these people?** Are they able to show emotions, or are they shut down emotionally?

- **Do they want you to take care of them or vice versa?** Are they needy or dependent themselves, or do they want you to fill those roles so they can take care of you?

- **Are they tightwads or generous?** Does every penny count to them and an item better be on sale if you purchase it, or are they always getting into financial scrapes because they don't pay attention to finances?

- **Do they criticize or support you?** Do you feel that others you bring into your life always find a way to put you down, or are they always there cheering you on in every area of your life?

You've answered these questions and can see the link to Mom confirming she has influenced your relationships. The good news is you now have the ammunition, by way of knowledge, to change your life around, and it's clear to you what threads you need to work on to have your very own life. You accomplish this by adopting new behaviors that depart from the mom gene, which slowly removes the pieces of her that you don't want. You are now on your way to achieving new goals and new ways of having relationships.

Now that you've found Mom in your relationships and have learned how to weed her out, we will look to see where she's lurking in your sexuality. It doesn't seem right that she's there also, but you'll see her by the messages she gave you about sex.

4

Mom as Sexual Sage

Joan was seven and had friends around her age who lived on her street. They would play together in the evenings and on weekends whenever any of them were home. One day, Joan and a neighbor girl and boy were in Joan's bedroom trying to think of something to do. The little boy said he would show the girls his private parts if they would show him theirs. They were all curious what everyone's genitals looked like, so they agreed, and removed their clothes and took turns looking at each other.

When the little boy was inspecting Joan's genitals, her mother walked into the room. Her mother, of course, sexualized the event and, shocked, blew her top. "What are you doing?" and "How dare you!" she screamed. She told them they were all "bad" children and she was going to tell their parents how "wicked" they were. She grounded Joan and told her she could not play with these friends ever again. Joan's mother, at that instant, passed on her mom gene in the sexual arena loud and clear—sex was bad, and therefore Joan got the message she was bad.

Mom's Messages About Sex

If Mom caught you "playing doctor" with the boy down the street and punished you, either verbally or physically, you are going to have a different view of sex than if she sat you down and explained the differences between boys and girls and what those differences mean. Some moms pass on healthy scripts in this area, but many don't understand all the components that go into making sex healthy and pleasurable. At least knowing what your mother's script was gives you a starting point on the road to a happy and healthy sex life all your own.

Whenever I talk to groups about sexuality I always ask where they learned about sex. When I ask if they learned anything about sex from their parents, only one or two hands go up. For most, books and peers were their main sources of information, while many individuals learned through personal experimentation.

I've had clients come in who know they have an issue with sexuality but are not ready to face what is amiss, so they leave and go out and re-create the same scenario. Some people do that all their lives, but for others it just takes another time or two and they realize they have to address the problem, because life is just too painful their old way.

If you, too, feel that your sex life could be more satisfying, for whatever reason, be a sleuth, put your cap and monocle on, and look at your mom with the clearest vision you can muster. See what she believed and why she gave you the messages she did. That's your ticket out of mom's sex beliefs.

Sex is the most fundamental part of life—how ironic it is that it's the very reason we exist, and yet many moms treat it as a dark little secret best left in the musty corners of the attic. They ignore its presence and play the game of, "Mother says don't talk or ask about sex. Let's pretend it doesn't exist." Instead, without even realizing it, Mom's silence actually screamed out messages about the value and role of sexuality in a woman's life.

Covert messages are like flashing neon signs that give statements about sex without even addressing the issue directly. One way this may occur is Mom making comments about sex in general, not linking it to either herself or her daughter, which allows her to keep the subject impersonal without addressing any feelings that tag along. Mom also sends messages about sex when she can't see beyond her own issues to address the complexity of sex without bias. As a result, she remains mute on the subject. Her daughter has to pick up whatever messages came out of her childhood, spoken or unspoken, and devise her own strategy for dealing with sex.

What Kind of Message Did You Get?
- Sex shouldn't be talked about.
- Sex shouldn't be really enjoyed.
- Sex shouldn't be experimental.
- Sex is normal and natural.
- You can manipulate through sex.
- You can be manipulated through sex.
- Nice girls don't.
- You can't trust anyone sexually.
- Sex is a wonderful experience.
- Men are only after one thing.
- It's all about them.
- Your body is not to be shared.
- You're not pretty enough or your figure isn't what it should be to attract a good man and enjoy healthy sex.
- Sex with its emotional component is one of life's pleasures.
- Sex is a game that you should win.
- Sex is a game that you should let him win.
- Sex with the right person is fulfilling.
- Sex is bad, and you're a bad person if you enjoy it.
- There's something wrong with sex or with your sexuality.

Many messages are given out by moms, and some get lost in translation. If you fear that you have a sexual hang-up that is negatively affecting your romantic relationships, this chapter will help you learn to identify which mixed messages you received and what to do about them to turn those old, worn-out messages around. You can feel like your own sexual person without Mom sitting on the bedpost telling you what's right and wrong, choreographing your every thought and move.

Some ways negativity about sex shows up could be the flinch when your honey shows even the slightest interest in watching a porn movie, or maybe you can't talk about sex to him, but you can to friends. Or maybe you experience some of these other telltale signs:

- You are able to joke about sex, but in the bedroom your body shuts down.
- You want more sex than your mate, and you hold this over his head.
- You have an affair and keep it hidden.
- You tease men, but don't want to follow through.
- You sexually service your partner but are uncomfortable receiving.
- You want all men to find you sexually attractive, because that's what boosts your self-confidence.
- You are too tired most of the time for sex.
- You have trouble reaching orgasm.
- You reach orgasm only to feel let down because now that it's over you have to have sex again in hopes you will feel something more.
- Your sex partner talks dirty and you are shocked to the core, or at least offended, and deem him inappropriate.
- You suspect you have a sex addiction.
- You are bored sexually and can't seem to get out of the rut even knowing your partner is a good lover.

These statements are indications that, in your life, sex has been corrupted in some way. It's either been diluted or overstressed and is not as fulfilling and pleasurable as it could be. Believe it or not, these deeply intimate feelings and outlooks about sex stem from your operating under the falsehood of the mom gene. The goal is to identify how your mom mismanaged sex so that you can change your sexual outlook and enjoy a healthy sexual give-and-take leading to a happy sex life all your own.

When a mother can't communicate about sex, and would prefer to keep it impersonal or something that other people do, she leaves a daughter no choice but to figure out how she will define or use sex and what her own feelings and thoughts are about it. She may have picked up from the mom who was withdrawn or unresponsive that sex is taboo or "bad." She must turn Mom's silence on its head and investigate her own sexual life.

The daughter also picks up unspoken ideas about sex by observing what Mom wears, how she moves her body, and how she relates to men. If Mom dressed in a provocative way, her daughter may pick up the message that sex is used to get attention from men, and her daughter may carry this on. She may use sex as a weapon and take any emotional connection out of the equation. If Mom always dressed in sloppy sweats and old sneakers or was the type to button all blouses to the neck with skirts to the floor, her daughter may have picked up the message that sex was not something to be enjoyed and explored but rather something to be hidden and maybe even to be fearful of.

If Mom was comfortable with her body and used it as a vehicle of pleasure, perhaps through some physical activity, her daughter learns that her own body is something to take joy in; if Mom held tension in her body, did not like to be touched, or abused her body in any way, her daughter subconsciously picks up the message that her physical self isn't important, which diminishes sexual pleasure.

If Mom was flirty with men, sex becomes a narcissistic game. If she always put her husband down or perhaps men in general, or was cold to them and treated them as if they were inconsequential, sex was conveyed as something trivial, and it certainly didn't have any warmth connected to it.

The conflicts then begin, much to the daughter's detriment. What could have been a wonderful part of life has now become an area rife with misunderstanding and misinformation, and the conflicts are left to the daughter to sort out.

To know and value your sexual self, you must first start with Mom's spoken judgments or unspoken subtle messages on the subject. Only then can you start to throw off her sex gene and work toward *your* version of a healthy sexuality. Try to focus on the basics for healthy sex: the ability to comfortably talk about sex and all its forms to your mate and to your children, appropriate for their stage of development; a comfort level with your body; the ability to sexually give and receive and an enjoyment of both; an understanding of how your own body works and a willingness to learn about your partner's body; and an acceptance of your sexuality and a clear desire to keep negative emotions out of it. From there you can add whatever touches you like to spice it up or make it more romantic or challenging or whatever it is your heart desires.

No-Win Mother Sexual Styles

Working with my clients on sexuality, large emotional components kept surfacing. Hidden feelings of fear, insecurity, resentment, or anger arose as sexual issues could be traced, in part, back to Mom and her sexual messages.

Daughters are exposed to Mom's particular belief system regarding sexuality, and all of its facets, from birth on. This programming starts way before a daughter's own sexual self starts to emerge. Whatever Mom's sexual message was, it had an incredible impact on her daughter's burgeoning sexuality—whether the gist was positive or negative.

The picture of sexuality Mom gives is influenced by her feelings of her own sexuality. She is unable to step out of herself and have an objective point of view on the subject and therefore is unable to give you an unprejudiced portrayal of sex. How she viewed sex is part of your sexuality that you carry around that may need flushing out. It's like getting an oil change for your car. You flush out the old fluid and replace it with fresh, new oil; it's the same with Mom's notions about sex. You need to flush out her views and put your new ones in.

I have identified seven different sexual styles in which a daughter's sexuality is compromised. The following list shows these various types of sexual messages you might have received from Mom and how they affected your sexuality, thus preventing you from having a healthy sex life.

Some of these types have very serious consequences, and some seem to be more benign, but in fact, few of us had sexually healthy role models growing up. The effect on our sexuality is clear, but the good news is we can change what we don't want any longer and start moving forward to a happy, satisfying sexuality all our own.

When you look at the different moms in this area, see if yours had just a smidgen of this or a smattering of that or if she was a full-blown Technicolor representative of the worst of the lot. Most moms do give their daughters the sexual picture they believe is correct, but sometimes it's not in their daughters' best interest. Don't blame Mom, but recognize her fingerprints all over your sexuality, and once you have identified which are hers and which ones you'd like for your own you can start to unravel the grip of her sexual convictions and become your own sexual being.

1. The Sexually Passive Mother. The daughter of the Sexually Passive Mother views sex as an obligation, so she builds up resentment against her mate for expecting her to engage in sex when she'd really rather not. She develops an attitude of coldness and physical isolation. Mom can be totally neutral about sex, as it's a nonentity to her and she doesn't see any value in it. She passes this mindset to her daughter. Or a daughter can go in the opposite direction and engage in promiscuity to prove Mom wrong.

2. The Sexually Expressive Mother. This mom teaches her daughter that sex is an abusive weapon to be used against everyone, including herself. She manipulates men through sex while ignoring the emotional component. This daughter either uses men for her own agenda or distances herself physically from sex. This daughter's pleasure comes from sexual power and control, but not from sex itself as she has depersonalized sex.

3. The Sexually Critical Mother. She gives the message that sex is an activity only for those on the lowest rung of the ladder. Sex becomes riddled with negativity and is therefore something to be avoided. There is nothing to look forward to in this area. Mom's judgmental nature gets passed on, and this daughter becomes judgmental herself and can feel she is bad for having sexual feelings.

4. The No-Sexual-Boundaries Mother. A lack of trust is fostered in this mother-daughter relationship, perpetrated by Mom acting as a competitor. As a result, the daughter brings to the sex table insecurities, anxieties, and fears preventing her from allowing total sexual pleasure. This leaves her to either be lacking in healthy sexual boundaries herself, or she shuts and locks the door to her sexuality.

5. The Sexually Interfering Mother. This mother badly wants to be her daughter's "friend," wants to hear about her daughter's sexual exploits, and thrives on all the details. Her daughter has no sense of partnerships in her life with friends, coworkers, relatives, or even her own children. She looks to her mate to judge her sexual performance and has no self-confidence in this area, or she may

be the one in command judging him. Mom's narcissistic expectation was that her sexuality was supposed to be her daughter's
sexuality.

6. The Sexually Insecure Mother. This mother doesn't feel
secure in her ability to attract a mate, so she uses her own daughter
as bait, leaving this daughter confused and distrusting of the meaning and purpose of sex. The daughter can try to be happy sexually,
but there is always something inside of her blocking the way because
she has learned detachment. She believes the true value of sex is how
you look and act.

7. The Sexually Abusive Mother. This mother inappropriately uses her daughter for her own sexual pleasure. By doing this
she promotes the idea to her daughter that sex has no emotional
connection, but is instead only a physical reaction. For her daughter, attaching emotions to sexual pleasure is a sign of weakness, and
the pleasure she does get is from a power and control base. The
daughter remains emotionally absent from sex and conflicted about
it. She has rules to keep the emotions in check, and does lots of com-
partmentalization in this area. A daughter not being comfortable
receiving sexual pleasure is a sign of this mom.

How your mother dealt with men gives you a template for your
own sexual dealings with men. She might have revered men, or she
might have had disdain for them; but however she looked at them
forms the basis for your interactions with the men in your life. What
you were exposed to sexually also governs your own sexuality.

The Sexually Passive Mom

This mother defines sex as an obligation. She feels it is her duty to
be sexual with her husband even though she would just skip that

part of life and act like it didn't exist if it were up to her. She had been taught that sex was a duty of being a wife and she must perform her conjugal duties no matter what she was feeling or how much or how little she enjoyed sex. It was something to subject herself to and, like a compliant wife not seeing any value in sex, do the right thing by her husband. To her it seemed easier to just lie there than to discover what all the fuss was about.

The Sexually Passive Mom believes there is no sexual pleasure for a woman. This is the sexual legacy that good old passive Mom passes onto her unsuspecting daughter by showing her the wife's role in a relationship is to acquiesce to all of her husband's demands and play the supportive role in their marriage. She has no identity of her own, and if she doesn't have it in the living room she sure doesn't have it in the bedroom. Children are smarter than a lot of people give them credit for, and this daughter was able to put two and two together and see what four looked like.

The idea that pleasure from sex is supposed to be only for the man leaves the daughter with the royal proclamation—with official seal—that women are only to be viewed as sex objects, because sex is for the man's pleasure. For this daughter her attractiveness to a man is based on *his* needs, *his* physical attraction to her, and if she is alluring enough to bring *him* to climax every time they have sex. Those are her responsibilities, and the ball is always in her court to tempt, tease, flirt with, and seduce him in any way she can.

The message clearly states that women are not valued for their intelligence, their abilities, or any number of other attributes they may have. It simply boils down to sex. Give men what they want sexually, don't take any personal sexual pleasure, and you've got the man/woman thing all worked out. Or so Mom believes. The legacy she has really left her daughter is one of feeling inferior in a partnership. She can be in the role of a second-class citizen, which further erodes any self-assuredness she might have had at one time.

Mom might still get her "screw yous" in, but it will come out in a passive-aggressive manner, still leaving her feeling second-rate because she never challenges her mate head-on.

This mom may put sex in the category of, "if you don't acknowledge sex, it doesn't exist." She never makes advances but instead always waits for her mate to initiate sex or any public displays of affection. She is not really comfortable with physical displays of affection even with her daughter, thus giving the message that physical contact isn't all that important. The daughter, then, afraid or shy about asking questions of Mom or gaining a healthy understanding of sex, its purpose, and its relation to her body, is left to her own devices to determine these issues on her own. Ultimately, a confused, repressed idea of sex develops.

The Sexually Passive Mom could easily have drifted so far away from her husband that he wasn't interested in sex with her anymore either. If only one person is getting satisfaction from sex it eventually becomes boring to both. Most people want something coming back from their partner so it's not just a "going through the motions" experience. If this is the case, they may decide, after years of marriage, that separate bedrooms are the way to go on the pretense that they would sleep better that way.

Even when they did both sleep in one bed, an invisible wall probably was erected right down the middle, distancing them from each other—if not physically then emotionally. This carries over into the daytime, and the parents' level of intimacy and trust in daily situations becomes nonexistent. Given the stand she has taken on sex, a sexually repressed mom has nothing in the way of positive sexual information or feelings to give her daughter. If the daughter has internalized Mom's message she is required to adopt the same "no sex is good sex" attitude or be out on a limb trying to get through the sex maze with no guidelines to help her sort out her own feelings and attitudes.

If she accepts her mom's sex gene, this daughter also waits for advances and puts herself in the position of having a spouse who says the classic, "How come you never make the first move?" She may know that to be true but can't seem to change. Another symptom of this mom gene is being uncomfortable with public displays of affection. On the flip side this daughter may rebel out of curiosity and disdain and become promiscuous, careless, and want in no way to give up on sex like Mom did. She doesn't look like Mom, on the surface anyway, but it's like looking in a mirror. She's the spitting image of her mom, just an opposite view.

BARBARA

Barbara grew up in a middle-class family with a mom and a dad and an older brother. She was very gregarious which, she discovered as she got older, attracted many men to her. She would go out to the trendiest nightclubs to dance, and if a man didn't ask her to dance, she'd ask him without a second thought and would spend the whole evening on the dance floor.

She wanted someday to have a husband and family, but right now she just wanted to meet men and the more the merrier. Her mother was a typical Sexually Passive Mom, so Barbara was more than confused as to the role that sex played in her own life even though she thought she had it all figured out.

She did what many women do and went to the opposite extreme of her mom's sexual passivity. Barbara had sex with whoever was handy and available at the moment with little thought to pregnancy or disease prevention. There was no way she was going to be like her mother and give up on sex. She thought she might as well join a nunnery if she wasn't going to have sex in her life. She didn't want to end up like Mom with children she really didn't know what to do with and a docile husband. No, gosh darn it; she was going to live differently.

When Barbara did have one of her many sexual encounters it seemed to be less than wonderful. It was okay, but every time she had sex, she heard her mother's voice saying, "This is all a man wants from you, so just lie there and let him have his pleasure, don't enjoy it." When a sexual partner offered her some pot, Barbara accepted and found that her mother's voice couldn't be heard any longer. She could now enjoy sex on her own without her mom being present, at least in her head.

Barbara rebelled so strongly against her mother's view of life and the way her mom delegated sex to the back page that she started experimenting with more and more drugs. They helped her shut out the doubt about her sexuality so that she could enjoy sex. The drugs and alcohol gave her an "I don't care" attitude, so soon she was using them on a pretty consistent basis. When she found herself pregnant, she didn't even know the ethnicity of the child's father. Time would tell, she would joke.

After giving her situation some serious thought, she decided she'd better clean up her act for both herself and her unborn child and so went into rehab and got clean. Then the work really began. She joined a support group and started hearing other people talk about their sexuality, which was so different from hers. She learned that her mother really and truly didn't have the final word in regard to sexuality. As a child, she thought her mom was the be-all and end-all authority on everything—and because she had no one to compare her mom to, she was left with Mom's messages and perceptions of sex.

Daughters of Sexually Passive Moms are often conflicted about their sexuality. They don't know what they are supposed to do with their sexual feelings and have no one to tell or even talk to about the inconsistency between what they feel and what they've been taught. It's a tough place to be in.

These daughters may be educated, sophisticated, and worldly, and you'd never guess that underneath they have no self-identity. They can have a depressive quality about them because of the feelings of low self-worth brought about by the conflict between their feelings and Mom's memorandums. They can be very accommodating in relationships because that's what they were taught, or they can jump to the other side and have to be in total charge so they are not vulnerable. Both ends of the candle are the product of low self-esteem.

Having this type of mom often leaves you feeling guilty because you have sexual feelings that Mom says you aren't supposed to have. From there, it's only logical for you to assume that something is wrong with you. This, of course, is going to show up in your relationships with partners. You and your partner can't grow together in intimacy, in trust, or sexually while you still believe you are not a person who has value.

WHAT TO DO. If you had such a mother, her voice might be loud and unmistakably reverberating in your head, or it can be just a vague rumbling. Either way it's there and will remain locked into place until it gets delegated to the trash bin labeled Mom's Erroneous Sex Beliefs. Admitting this voice is there is the way to start from scratch, and only then can you begin finding out exactly what *your* sexuality is all about, sans Mom. It sounds easy, but it's a lifelong discovery as one's sexuality is ever flowing and changing.

Recognize that the sexual role model you had in Mom was not a trustworthy one. You now need to find a role model who is more grounded and realistic about sexuality and start wiping the slate clean of what Mom believed. Depending on how deep this belief from Mom got into your head and heart and how much trouble you are having in this area, this new role model can be a friend or even a therapist, if need be. If you have a friend who is truly satisfied in her relationship and/or has a healthy sex life, think about how the two connect and complement each other. If you have a male friend who is deeply in love and want to hear a man's perspective, ask him for his point of view and connection with his mate. Then you can replace what you got from Mom with other, healthier points of view.

To move away from Mom's beliefs you must learn your value in and out of bed. Yes, it's true that many men like to be with a partner who is sexy to them, but a lot of men also like knowing that their partner has a brain and self-confidence, so work on all parts of you.

Start by confronting the negative messages that keep popping up in your head and replace them with "I respect and value my sexuality." Read all you can about sex and maybe take a human sexuality class at your local college. This class is very enlightening and educational, and you will come away with a different perspective on sex. If you don't know what works for your body sexually, become acquainted with your body and its sexual responses. If you do know your sexual body, tell yourself that your responses are healthy. Be sure to connect your emotions, noting how you are feeling every step of the way, to your physical sensations so that you can be a total sex diva. It's all yours for the taking, if you invest the time to get to really know your sexual self.

The Sexually Expressive Mom

You might think that the Sexually Expressive Mom would be a great mom to have in the sex arena. She's free and open with her sexuality, doesn't hide a thing, talks about it openly, and will offer her knowledge about sex without even being asked by her daughter. This may sound like an ideal upbringing, but there's a catch. This is all about Mom's view of sex and does not take into account the effect her actions are having on her daughter's sexuality, which is the downside to all of these no-win sexual styles. Mom has it all figured out, and her daughter better do it the way Mom says, as *it's the right way*, don't you know?

If you experienced this type of mom, sex became all about Mom, leaving you without a guide in the sexual area. In addition, you had a premature exposure to sex, which brought a lot of baggage to the mix. The message was that sex is the dominant theme in life and that it is mystical and important without any explanation of what goes with it. Sex became inflated and overloaded without the emotional part being considered. Mom's self-worth was based on whether she got any sex or not and how often. It was as if she measured herself by the notches on her bedpost.

There was a misuse of sex, as sex was seen as a force to be reckoned with and so it was depersonalized. Attaining sexual pleasure was all about power and control and had little to do with the actual sex act. Mom thought she had men and sex all figured out and was quite proud of that fact and even bragged about her so-called power and control over men.

When a mother talks in sweeping generalities, saying, in this case, that all men can be manipulated through sex by a female, if she just knows what she is doing, you, as a daughter, can't tell the difference between what your mother is saying and what the truth is about men, women, and sex. Sex becomes loaded, and it loses its individualization. The result is a daughter going to extremes in adolescence, either sleeping with everyone in sight or being the pristine virgin and not even allowing a kiss good night.

PAULA

Paula was a successful businesswoman who owned her own clothing store and seemed to be balanced in other areas of her life. She exercised regularly, visited with friends and family when she could, had one divorce behind her, and was living with another man. On the surface it all looked good, but underneath trouble was brewing. She had to be in charge of everything in her life, which included sex with her live-in love. Of course, her being in total charge of their sex life was getting in the way and preventing the intimacy she really wanted because, in her view, sex was only to fulfill her desire and the heck with his.

Growing up, Paula was exposed to her mother's handling of sex in a way that damaged her own budding sexuality. There was no doubt that Mom was a sexual being. Everyone in the house was quite aware of that fact. Her mom dressed provocatively and flirted with her husband every chance she got. Sexual innuendoes were always running between her parents, and once their bedroom door was closed her mom was unavailable for the duration of the sexual encounter whether it was fifteen minutes or three hours.

Night after night, Paula heard sex sounds coming from her parents' bedroom, and there was nothing she could do to drown them out. If any of the children needed a drink of water, got scared of the dark, or just wanted a hug from Mom, that was too bad, she was engaged in sex. For Paula's mom, sex was more important than anything or anyone else, and it occurred to Paula that sex was running her mom's life and as a consequence, her own life.

When Paula's parents divorced—all that sex didn't keep the marriage intact—her mother met a new man and spent whole weekends at his place, leaving her children home alone. At a young age Paula decided she wasn't going to let anyone or anything have control over her the way her mother had done. She was going to be the one in control at all times.

The form this took in her current relationship was that she and her boyfriend had separate bedrooms, and it was understood that Paula would come into his bed when she wanted sex and leave afterward to return to her own bedroom. She was in control to the max, but at the same time realized this was the legacy left by her mother's involvement with sex. Paula had been in therapy in the past, but to date hasn't wanted to delve into the way sex is still controlling her life and preventing her from living the life she would like to have.

The daughter of a Sexually Expressive Mom received erroneous messages about sex and is confused about its role in life. This daughter doesn't know if she should manipulate men like Mom did or allow the tables to be turned and permit someone to manipulate her. Mom's misuse of sex allowed it to become depersonalized, so either way works for her. Because the daughter saw her mother use sex as a manipulation tool, she thinks that's part of the game plan.

For this daughter, pleasure comes from sexual power and control and not from sex itself. She has learned that the power and control base for sex is the most important and most rewarding. That way, she keeps sex depersonalized and uses it against others. The problem is that she misuses sex and ends up using the abusive weapon of sexual power and control against herself also, as she gets no satisfaction from sex itself.

These daughters can be overly involved with family as they feel insecure and want to prove they are worthwhile to Mom and get her sanction. If Mom would put her stamp of approval on her daughter's way of living and her sexual choice, the daughter could feel valuable. Another coping mechanism these daughters can use is to look the other way and put family at the bottom of the list, sending the message that they don't care about what Mom thinks. This way they don't risk the chance of Mom's disapproval overtly, even though they live with it in their heads. They've detached from their family with the mind-set, "I'm going to reject you before you can criticize me again." Consequently, because they are still react-

ing to the mom gene, other relationships in their lives are not satisfying either. Whatever the surface appears to be, underneath these
daughters are floundering.

What to Do. If your mom fits the picture of the Sexually Expressive Mom, you have steps to take to disentangle her beliefs about sex
from a more realistic view of sexuality. Mom believes that sex is a
weapon, a notion that you have to get out of your mind. First, you
need to closely look at your mom and all the sexual messages she
loaded you down with. Make a list of how these messages manifested
in her life. Look to see if she talked differently when on the phone
with her partner or acted differently in his presence. Perhaps she
dressed differently when he was expected. Maybe she talked about
him all the time and bragged about how she controlled and manipulated him sexually. Next, look to see if you have done the same
with various partners you have had.

Put your sexuality on the back burner for a moment and relate to
men in general and/or your partner on a different level. With sex
out of the picture, think about what you have to offer a man. If you
are fun to be with; can carry on an intellectual conversation; are
good at social events; are calm, patient, and understanding; or have
financial savvy or any other attribute aside from sex, make note of
that. Use those skills and talents in your relationship, and leave sex in
the bedroom where it belongs. If you've been making all the sexual
moves, stop and let him approach you. Tell your partner you would
enjoy his taking the initiative.

However, if you've always been a sexual wallflower, come out
from the corner and take some control back. Tell your mate you are
practicing being half of the sexual partnership and you are looking
for equality with all the bells and whistles you can muster up.

In either case, start identifying the emotional component to sex—
what your mood is, how you are feeling about your partner both on
the surface and deep inside of you. Also look at yourself and deter-

mine how you feel about yourself, first generally and then more specifically. This will help you gain freedom from lugging the mom gene forward so you can be you in every area of your life—a wonderful person both in and out of the sack.

The Sexually Critical Mom

This mother just simply closes the door, shuts down, and bids a fond farewell to her sexuality. She doesn't have to face its existence, but rather can just walk away from sex with her head held high. She's quite proud that she has risen above sex and feels very noble that she doesn't get bogged down by sexual desire or need to participate in such an experience. She's above it all. She has far more important areas in her life to deal with, and her daughter should heed Mom's warning and shut the sex door also. In fact, she believes *everyone* should.

The Sexually Critical Mom is very judgmental. She has judged sex to be beneath the truly righteous person, and since she has declared herself to have the most honorable morals of anyone, you better do it her way.

Remember, this mom has already deemed herself the all-knowing wise woman of all times, and if you dare to question her decrees you are wrong, and every nice thing she said about you is now officially taken back. Often, a negative, aggressive energy comes from this mom in many areas. Whether you received this type of energy and took it in or you let it bounce off determines what you do with your own sexuality.

If you have internalized this negative energy, you could be critical of your own sexual desires. You may begin to wonder about and doubt your own sexual feelings and may assume you're bad for having them. On the other hand, if you let Mom's judgment bounce off because you didn't buy into her perceptions, you are better equipped to explore your sexuality at your own pace.

These moms talk a good talk and give information to their daughters as though it were the gospel truth, but the conversations between mom and daughter regarding men and sexuality don't always tell the truth. These moms don't talk to their daughters about what men are like and what they are good at. Instead, Mom talks to her daughter about how to manipulate, control, and dominate men. The daughter has no sense of accomplishment in growing together with a mate in intimacy and trust because she wasn't given the proper perspective.

Instead the message could be, "All men are like this" and "All women are like that," which impersonalizes sexuality. If you take in generalities like "Sex is for sluts" or "Men will leave you once you give them what they want sexually," *and* your mother doesn't take into account your feelings on these treatises, you have just been handed a distorted thesis on sex.

This mom judges and criticizes in many ways, so you have to look for the judgments coming from her on any and every subject and recognize that's all that they are—judgments, not fact. Soon these judgments will become clearer, enabling you to see all the generalities Mom made up to get through life and to control those around her.

ELLEN

Ellen was a man pleaser, and it had started with her father. Growing up she did what she could to gain Dad's attention and love and was always happy when they went places together, just the two of them. They had a nice understanding between them, and Ellen loved to light up her father's face with one of her jokes or accomplishments.

On the other hand, Ellen's mom didn't much like her husband, but she did like the financial security that marriage afforded her. Mom knew how to play the marriage game and

did it well. She knew how to keep her husband at least some-
what satisfied, and he was content to just go through life relying on his wife's control. It seemed to be easier to let her run
the show because that is what his father had done. It was very
clear—the female was in charge.

Mom was Ellen's role model in being female, and Ellen saw
the manipulating that went on from Mom to Dad. Liking her
dad and yet seeing how her mother got her way with him left
a mishmash of contradictions for Ellen. She wanted to be herself and have people like her for herself, but it looked like the
way to be womanly and get her needs met was by controlling
those around her.

When she met Steve she had been on the dating scene for
a while and had had a few lovers along the way. She always
seemed to like sex better than her lovers did and to be better
at it than they were. Oh sure, they liked sex, but she wanted the
whole kit and caboodle—engaging in lots of foreplay and teasing, experimenting with new places and positions, watching
X-rated videos, and making her own movies. These past lovers
seemed to be attracted to her sexuality, but it always turned out
to be because they weren't sexually free themselves and wanted
her to lead them down this exciting new path. She grew tired
of always being the one in charge, but that was the type of men
she chose. She had learned well from Mom.

Steve was married when Ellen met him, but that didn't stop
her from making a play for him. She was ready to settle down
with someone, and since the previous married man she had
been involved with left his wife for her, she figured Steve
would also. Getting a married man to choose her meant she
had value over another woman.

Ellen gave this budding relationship everything she had. She
welcomed Steve into her home wearing her sexiest clothes

when she opened the door, bought sex toys she knew he had never tried but would enjoy, found odd and risky places to have sex in, subscribed to sexy magazines so they could look at the photos together—whatever her mind could conjure up, she did. He, of course, thought he had died and gone to sex heaven, if there were such a place. This was his dream come true in all his sexual fantasies. His current wife didn't have a chance.

Soon Ellen and Steve were living together, but since he had children with his soon-to-be ex-wife, he wanted to stay in contact with them. He had not been raised to desert his children, so the drama started unfolding. Here he was, living with Ellen and seeing his children and their mother on a regular basis. Ellen was not happy with this arrangement, as she wanted Steve all to herself, and started pulling away from him.

She didn't buy any new toys, started sleeping in her T-shirt, and cooking dinner in the nude was out of the question. Steve was lucky at this point to have dinner waiting for him at all. Most of the time, Ellen was just too tired or was out with her girlfriends.

Ellen was disappointed that Steve wasn't participating in the relationship the way she wanted, so she did what she knew how to do—withhold sex—which put her back in charge of every situation. It was the same as saying through a bullhorn, "Do our relationship my way or you don't get sex. Take your pick, buddy boy."

Many daughters of Sexually Critical Moms dress in a provocative manner and either play innocent and wonder why men come on to them; or, they know exactly what they are doing and love the attention, for whatever it's worth. Other daughters couldn't be bothered with the subject of sex and come across as cold and rigid. Their moms may have used religion as a reason to avoid sex, and some daughters follow suit.

Judgment is always a part of these daughters' lives. They judge themselves and they judge others, and consequently judgment enters into all of their relationships. Such a daughter may judge her partner and punish him by withholding sex, or she may reward him sexually if he has done something she approves of.

If you grew up with a Sexually Critical Mom, you missed out on learning to accept others for who they are and allowing them to be just that. This includes sex as well as all other areas of life. Since Mom skipped over the warm, caring, understanding, and accepting part of relationships, you have a one-sided view of sexuality. But that can be rectified.

WHAT TO DO. Mom judged you in a lot of different areas and ways, but you can skip Mom's raised eyebrow or the disapproving purse of her lips regarding sex by simply looking the other way and not paying her any heed. To do this you must put aside her judgmental nature and start pursuing your own sexual path.

To start this process, if your mom is still in your life, make note to listen for these judgments coming from her and once you hear them take your mental eraser and obliterate every word. It's when you are not paying attention to what she is saying that her judgments slip in. If you listen or argue with her they also enter your head. Be on guard and refuse to let them enter at all. If she isn't in your life, listen to those judgments you hear inside of you, identify they are from Mom, and do the same trick with the eraser.

One judgment you might have about yourself may be about your body. You may judge it too skinny or too fat or too out of shape or you may have any number of concerns. You may not be able to enjoy sex without limits, as being physically self-conscious is a barrier to letting go and being in the moment. Instead, make friends with your body and recognize it for what it is. Stand in front of a mirror and tell yourself that you accept what you look like. You may want to change some parts, sure, but for right now you are who you are. Keep working on increasing your positive body image, and if you haven't in the past, start having sex with the lights on and undressing in front of your partner.

Now you can begin to change your outlook on sex, both internally and externally. Without judgment you can grow sexually. Invest some time listening to people you trust talk about sex. Take some classes or read books on a particular form of sex you'd like to explore. You can also see a sexologist for some help. Learn what sex is all about when there's no judgment attached. It's your game now, and you get to decide how it's going to be played.

The No-Sexual-Boundaries Mom

This mother can manifest her lack of boundaries in various ways. She might be overly friendly with her daughter's boyfriends so that her daughter senses the boyfriend "belongs to Mom." Perhaps this mom encourages a platonic relationship between herself and her daughter's boyfriend in the guise of, "I was just being nice to him because you like him" so that her daughter becomes confused and doesn't know if Mom is a competitor or a predator. She doesn't know where Mom's boundaries are. This daughter is reluctant to bring her boyfriend home because of the energy coming from Mom to him.

There is a series of boundaries that a mom can cross, and each brings with it a different set of problems for her daughter. If Mom flirts with her daughter's boyfriend and tries to compete for his attention, her daughter feels less safe and secure in her own sexuality. In the extreme, the No-Sexual-Boundaries Mom might actually have sex with the boyfriend, betraying the daughter and leaving her devastated and unable to trust even those closest to her.

Mothers with no sexual boundaries are more numerous than you might think, and you would never be able to spot them walking down the street. They can have great jobs and pleasing personalities, but a narcissistic personality lurks underneath the surface, which means the daughter can never trust her mother—in any area. The daughter wants to trust her mom, as we all do, but this mother is not to be relied on for anything.

Daughters try to believe they can trust their moms, at least where their personal sex life is concerned, but with this mother, the daughter can't be assured her mother will not cross a line in some way. Mom is only concerned with herself, you see, and nothing about her daughter is going to come in to spoil Mom's need. The world revolves around Mom, and her daughter exists only to give Mom what Mom wants.

The difficulty is that the No-Sexual-Boundaries Mom has a total lack of empathy and so *cannot* put herself in her daughter's place. This makes Mom untrustworthy in all areas. This mother, sad to say, needs immediate gratification and validation, and she will do anything to get it. There are no limits or boundaries, and her daughter pays a heavy price for her mother's lack of awareness. Mom's life is lived for the moment with no thought of how her actions are going to affect someone, including her daughter, in the next moment in time, let alone in the future.

Mom has such a great need to be liked that anything goes and nothing is off limits. That she might cross the line of decency in her daughter's sexual life is immaterial to her.

TINA

Tina was married, but she and her husband had a rocky and not very intimate relationship. They would have a fight and Tina would give her husband the cold shoulder, not talking to him for days. She only knew how to make her point by withdrawing and giving him the silent treatment. She would eventually start talking to him again, at least until the next time they had an argument. Then it was back to punishing him for something she believed he did wrong. Tina didn't know how to have a relationship that included communication, with each person being allowed to voice needs, wants, and desires, as Mom had never given her that template.

For most of Tina's life her mother had been a single parent and was always looking for her next boyfriend. Married or single, it didn't make much difference to Mom who was in her bed, as long as he was male. With the variety of men coming and going through Tina's life, she found it difficult to establish any sort of bond or trust with a man.

Her mother was the only resource Tina had when learning how to build truth and intimacy in relationships. Since her mom didn't know either, Tina was lost in a sea of uncertainty when it came to forming a relationship that would make her happy.

Tina and her mom had always had a tempestuous time together, but the clincher in their relationship came when Tina discovered that her mom had slept with one of her old boyfriends. What a kick in the stomach that was.

Apparently, one day Tina's old boyfriend had come over to say hi to her mom, and true to form, Tina's mom began flirting with him. One of Mom's questions to men was always, "Are you good?" which let the man know she was not only sexually available, but also primed and ready to give him the time of his life. This sexual prowess was Mom's only goal, and it validated her without a thought about how this action would affect her daughter.

Tina, of course, was devastated, and after yelling, crying, and screaming at her mother she told her she never wanted to see or talk to her again. Tina went into therapy and learned how her mother's behavior throughout her life had influenced her own sexuality and relationships with men. Tina's choice of a husband was someone who didn't much care for sex either, and neither one of them had much trust in that area. They were a wounded pair, and it showed up in their sex life. If they barely touched on sexual intimacy they got scared and backed off, not having sex for months on end. Then sex would slowly come back until the next time. They didn't know it yet, but over time sex would disappear entirely.

Sexual intimacy was a place Tina didn't want to go to because the silent, unrecognized question was always, "Would he have sex with someone else, including my mother?" She knew she couldn't trust her mother, and maybe she couldn't trust her husband either.

Daughters of the No-Sexual-Boundaries Mom are usually unable to make decisions because of their deep-rooted feelings of inferiority and inability to trust themselves enough. When they have to make a decision, they ask five different people their opinions before deciding what to do. Trust doesn't come easily to these daughters, so they can become detached from not only themselves, but those around them also. They may give lip service to friendships, but the trust really isn't there.

On the other hand, if they do decide to have a relationship they usually choose someone who is even less sure of himself than they are. This daughter may decide one thing and change her mind the next day or week or month, while her partner just ignores her and goes about his business as detached from her and she is from him.

Fears are often a part of their lives, which can take the form of feeling afraid of being home alone at night to never walking under a ladder or allowing a black cat to cross their path. Fears and anxieties oftentimes rule their lives, sometimes subtly and sometimes overtly.

These daughters can be promiscuous, or they can shut down their sexuality at any point in their lives and live a celibate life, or at least a sexually tenuous one. Sex is never easy and free because the trust issue keeps resurfacing no matter how hard they try to say it isn't so.

WHAT TO DO. Realizing that the No-Sexual-Boundaries Mom impacts your own sexuality is the first step toward getting your own life back and realizing the potential you had before Mom corrupted it with her issues.

When you have acknowledged Mom's part in how you feel about and deal with your sexuality the next step is to explore your personal sexuality. Leave Mom out of the equation and begin focusing on the sensual side of your being. This time how you feel does count, and the uplift that comes from this realization boosts your self-esteem to wonderful heights. It's a great way to be in the world.

Experience your sensuality through all of your senses: touch, taste, smell, sight, and sound. Notice if silk or any other material feels good against your body, and enjoy the feeling. If there is particular music that touches you, note that and stay in that moment as long as you can. Determine what some of your favorite fragrances are and have those around you. Look to see what sight makes you feel sensuous: maybe it's a sunset or a painting or a running brook. For many women, chocolate is sensuous, or maybe it's fruit. Determine what your sensuous foods are.

Learn to trust yourself and your own feelings. If you make a mistake, that's all right, we all make them. The trick is to learn from them and move on. Work on trusting your sexual feelings and responses both with yourself and with your mate. If he accepts and respects your newfound sexual expression, believe him and build on that.

You are now learning about your sexuality and can move forward increment by increment, feeling more and more comfortable sharing all parts of you with another person.

The Sexually Interfering Mom

This mother has an unaccountable interest in and encouragement of her daughter's sexuality. She wants to hear all about her daughter's first kiss, her first masturbatory experience, the first time a boy touches her breasts, and she wants to know all about her first orgasm. Nothing is off limits for this mom. She thrives on hearing all the details and isn't shy about asking for and demanding a play-by-play report.

The daughter of this mom tries to please her mother by sharing all of her sexual secrets, only to be taken down by Mom when she does and accused of sexual wickedness. It's quite a contradiction coming from Mom and totally confusing to her daughter. The daughter is trying to make Mom happy and have Mom acknowledge that she's a good daughter, telling her what she thinks she wants to hear, yet Mom turns the tide and uses what her daughter has shared against her.

Mom's insecurities can make her into a bully or cause her to adopt an "I'm better than you" attitude to make her feel better about herself, so the daughter is left with not being able to win no matter what she does. If she doesn't share her sexuality with Mom, she gets berated for keeping secrets from the one who loves her the most, and when she does tell her mom all, she is tossed to the lions and chastised for being sexually immoral. On one hand Mom appears to want to be her daughter's friend, and then all of a sudden she switches back into the role of Mom. Back and forth Mom goes, making her daughter a puppet of her own momentary needs. This is narcissism at its finest.

It's no wonder this daughter is so conflicted in the area of sex. She's damned if she does and damned if she doesn't. Taken into an adult sexual relationship this mind-set causes all kinds of havoc. She's afraid to tell the man she's with what her sexual interests and fantasies are, and yet feels like she has to tell him everything. She can choose a man who is also going to berate her for her sexual feelings or past experiences just like Mom did when she was growing up.

Or she can choose someone who lets her run the show and doesn't question her sexuality or anything else about her. Either being submissive or dominant in a relationship renders it out of balance. She sure didn't receive a sense of partnership in any form from Mom, so either way she goes the result is a lack of an equal partner.

CAROL

Carol was an attractive but unassuming woman. She had never believed she could personally be in a position of authority, so she always had jobs where she was subordinate. She was a good employee, although slow in her tasks. She was meticulous and would go over and over her work to make sure there were no mistakes. Watching her work made fellow employees want to pull their hair out.

Carol was the mother of two preteen boys and had been married to the same man for eighteen years. He was very insecure and checked up on what Carol did all the time, thinking she might be having an affair. When she was out of the room he would go through her purse to see if he could find any incriminating evidence.

This doubting of his had started soon after they married. He wanted to know her past sexual experiences, and when she shared them with him, he seemed to take it all in. After a while he didn't ask any more questions but started throwing back to her the details she had shared. If she had those experiences before him, surely she was oversexed, not to be trusted, and she would do it again, was his reasoning.

Carol thought she had found someone who was really interested in who she was as a person, but instead found he just wanted the information about her past to take her down a peg or two so he could be the powerful one in their relationship. Her husband, just like her mom, had an "I'm better than you" attitude. Carol had lived with that as a child and is living with it again now as an adult.

At this point Carol can't seem to break the tie she has with her husband because she has been dependent on him, believing, just like she did with Mom, that to be a good person she must do anything to please him. She had lived with her mother's interference in her personal life, so it wasn't a stretch for her to live it again with her husband. This was all she knew, and in a lot of ways the situation was comfortable since she knew what to expect from her husband's prying and how to handle the criticism that came with that.

Carol toned down her sexual responses and any spontaneity she might have liked to express so that she would not run the risk of being chastised for her wantonness. Of course, her husband reprimanded her for her lack of sexual energy and involvement, so there was always a push/pull between them. As he pushed for more from her sexually, she pulled away to the same degree. She would rather he have the image of her as a sexual slug than be accused of being a whore.

Daughters of Sexually Interfering Moms have conflicts around sexuality that impede on their whole life, not just in that one area. These conflicts can result in physical problems and emotional issues, and show up in their professional lives, with their children, and in all other relationships. To have to second-guess your mother's or partner's response, as Carol did, is very stressful. Physiologically, daughters can feel sick to their stomachs, have headaches or problems with elimination. They generally have an uneasiness about them. Because they feel they have to pick the lesser of two evils, depression and identity crises emerge.

On the other hand, this daughter, knowing only narcissism from Mom, oftentimes develops partnerships with those who permit this type of behavior from her and allow life to be centered on her. Other times she attracts those who are self-absorbed themselves because she's been there and done that and knows what's expected of her.

If this was your mom, you may lack self-confidence, as you were never allowed to develop a sense of self away from Mom. You could always be looking to others to tell you who you are. You have become skilled at being dependent on outer validation rather than checking in with yourself first. Sexually, there is a naïveté; your body is there, but your mind and emotions are left outside the bedroom door because Mom deemed them unimportant, and so you never learned how to connect your body with your mind and emotions.

What to Do. The good thing about this mother is that her sexual interference was so blatantly clear and out in the open that it's easy to see where the damage came from. It's not as subtle as other sexually misinformed mothers, and so you have the advantage in already knowing where your issues came from.

Your job is to take it from there and do the work to loosen your mom's grip on your sexuality. Make a list of what you deem as acceptable and unacceptable sexual practices. Perhaps you believe that "good" girls don't touch their genitals, or you think that talking sexually is akin to being a porn star. Examine your list and see if you consciously believe that to be true today or if it's a carryover from Mom's involvement in your sexuality.

Try on different sexual scenarios in your head and pay attention to what happens in your body. If they arouse pleasant feelings or sexual excitement they are your feelings, but if your mind jumps in and says, "Whoa, better watch out, you are crossing the line into being a whore," they are your mom's. If you get both body and mind signals, tell your mind you are just trying this on for size to see if it fits for your sexuality and will decide later if you want to move forward with it or not.

If you decide you do want to move ahead, you have to go outside your comfort zone and experiment. If you've never had sex with your eyes open or looked into your partner's eyes while you are having an orgasm, let yourself be vulnerable enough to try it. Always ask yourself the following questions: How do I feel? Did I enjoy it? Did I feel connected? How did my partner respond? You don't have to do it for the rest of your life if you don't like it, but you have nothing to lose by trying something new a few times. The only way to claim your sexuality as your own is to experiment with it. It's worth every step you have to take on the road of sexual healing to be able to experience your sexuality just as you were meant to before Mom got in the way.

The Sexually Insecure Mom

This mom doesn't want to be a mom. She has turned the mother-daughter relationship into a sister act by parading her daughter in front of men to get their attention. Since Mom's insecurities lead her to believe that she is incapable of attracting men on her own she uses her daughter as bait.

To her daughter it feels as if she is being pimped when she is being used in this way. No money exchanges hands, but the daughter is under her mother's care and so-called protection and has no other recourse but to do Mom's bidding. This daughter often feels sorry for Mom because she senses Mom's inadequacies and tries to take care of Mom by going along with her program. Mom has detached emotionally from men and sex and instead places value on how one looks and acts, since, in her mind, that is the only way to get a man. Presentation is everything to this mom. Forget depth.

A Sexually Insecure Mom uses her daughter to procure men, and she can start her down this path at any age. This type of mom can start using her daughter in this way when the daughter is as young as three, or it can start later when the child is eight or even older. The younger daughter can be told to come and do a dance or sing a song to this man, and while she's at it she should sit on his lap and give him a kiss. The daughter is instructed to play up to him and appeal to him so that he'll like Mom a whole bunch. Mom is teasing him with her daughter in hopes that she'll reap the benefit later.

If a daughter is older when Mom does this, perhaps it is because Mom's lifestyle has changed in some way. Maybe she's single now or has put on weight or somehow doesn't feel she has the means to attract men on her own or thinks she doesn't know how. She might dress her eight-year-old in provocative and sexy clothes and teach her daughter to slyly tempt any man that Mom is interested in so he feels like he's getting two for the price of one. The message is that he can have sex with Mom and have a young girl fawn all over him as well.

This becomes a role reversal, with the daughter mothering her mother and taking care of Mom's needs, disregarding her own. This mom is usually depressed or volatile, and it becomes clear to the child that life is all about Mom. This is a basic core betrayal for the daughter, as she is treated as a commodity, not as a person in her own right.

VICTORIA

Victoria didn't try to be sexy and, in fact, didn't really want to come across that way, but she had a sex appeal whether she was in sweats or dressed to the nines. Men always turned their heads when she walked by, and she always got the best treatment from male servers in restaurants. Victoria had been sexualized at a young age and the attention from men now turned Victoria off, but it hadn't always been that way.

Victoria grew up with an insecure mom who doubted her attraction to men. Her mom thought she needed an extra lure, so she used her daughter as that extra bonus for any man who came around. Victoria's hair was primped to fall into ringlets, and she was dressed in the cutest clothes her mother could find. She was a china doll to be lifted off the shelf and taken out when her mother felt she needed to impress a man. What male would not be thrilled he could get two females for the price of one? He could have a sexual relationship with a woman and the cutest little girl in the world to flatter him. Victoria and her mom were a package deal, and for some men, it was hard to resist.

Being treated as a commodity rather than a person, Victoria went through a phase in her adolescence and early twenties of using those same ploys to attract men. She knew how to interest men and used that for all it was worth. It worked, and Victoria became a promiscuous young women. She had the formula and used it to her advantage, or so she thought.

She would troll the nightclubs and became known on the scene as a cute, vivacious, easygoing girl who enjoyed a good time. The problem for Victoria came when she realized her moods swung from wanting to party all the time to being down in the dumps. There was no balance in her life, as she would go from highs to lows. She knew something was wrong, so she sought the help of a therapist. She stopped going to clubs and enrolled in school. Victoria was determined to find something else of value about herself aside from her ability to be a sex object.

At school she met and eventually married a man, despite the fact that she was now turned off of sex. She knew that sex was a part of marriage, so tried to make a point of once a week, on weekends, having sex with her husband. There were a lot of areas of sex she wasn't comfortable with, so their sexual repertoire was limited, but faithfully once a week they tried to enjoy sex. That it was less than wonderful for either of them soon became apparent, and they are now seeking another therapist to help them through their sex issue.

Neither Victoria nor her husband knows the first thing about trust and intimacy, so they have their work cut out for them. You can't have an emotionally satisfying, long-term sexual relationship without allowing yourself to be a bit vulnerable. In fact, you can't have a healthy relationship in any area without it.

If you grew up with this Sexually Insecure Mom your feelings of being just a product taints your interpretation of everything Mom does, resulting in a severe lack of trust in her. If she takes you out for a fancy meal for your birthday, you automatically assume it's for her to show off the ten pounds she just lost or so she can flirt with the waiter. You tend to generalize this mistrust and project it out to everyone else. You may have a hard time relating to other women, as your experiences have led you to believe women have ulterior motives for doing what they do. There is no way you could believe otherwise if you bought into your mom's behavior.

You have lost out on having your own sense of identity, sexually and otherwise. You may feel that you can't get the satisfaction out of sex that others talk about and don't understand what all the hoopla is about. Sex is sex, but you believe there's more to it than what you are experiencing, and you wonder what the heck is wrong with you. The issue here is that you don't want to be vulnerable as you've been shown that sex was a game for Mom and all the men she got involved with, so you are unconsciously holding back. Instead you live with a "going through the motions" sexual existence, having only a piece of the sexual pie.

What to Do. If you are willing to push your way through the sexual blocks you'll find change isn't as foreboding as it may appear to be. You have to keep repeating to yourself that Mom had her way in dealing with men and you, as an adult now, can have your own personal way. Her way was not a universal law and is open to your own interpretation and behavior.

Look at where you have detached in your life. Detachment usually brings limitations. For example, if you are not open to hearing another's opinion you lose out on connecting with that person and having more information than you had before. You can stay closed off and think you are safe from what you would feel is criticism, but you've also lost the opportunity to experience true intimacy with another person. Intimacy involves sharing your thoughts and feelings with another person, expecting an acceptance of your stance even if they don't agree, and allowing their feelings and thoughts to be equally important to you. When you have located your detachments, decide if you are willing to accept the limitations detachment brings.

You may feel vulnerable without your detachment, but realize that when you are vulnerable you don't have to accept attack or damage from another. You are simply expressing your feelings and seeing what the other does with what you've shared. If you share something personal with someone and he or she doesn't respect your feelings you can always withhold any further sharing in this area. Knowing when to give a part of yourself and when to withhold it leaves the power with you.

If you let go and have the best orgasm of your life and your partner thinks that's the greatest thing since the invention of the remote control, go for it, as you've just exposed yourself and it's been rewarded with positive feedback. On the other hand, if you have a mind-blowing climax and he ridicules you in any way, then or any time in the future, you know you aren't safe around him and you don't put yourself in that position with him ever again. It becomes your choice to be vulnerable or not.

The Sexually Abusive Mom

Historically, men were believed to be the perpetrators of sexual abuse and were thought to be the only ones who fell in this category. Nowadays, we know differently. Women as well as men are sexual abusers, and this abuse can take many different forms, including Mom as molester; Mom closing her eyes as her daughter, or anyone in the family, is being molested; Mom sharing her sexual exploits in detail with her daughter; or Mom being the watchdog and overly concerned with her daughter's growing sexuality.

If she is indeed the sexual perpetrator this can be under the pretext of showing her daughter "how good it feels when Mom rubs you like this." Her abuse is performed under the guise that she is teaching her daughter about sex. When the daughter is grown and gets sexual satisfaction without Mom, either by herself or with men, Mom gets jealous, as she's been replaced. Her daughter is confused because Mom was teaching her, and when she begins to approach sex on her own, Mom no longer likes her. Where once she was emotionally connected, at this point she disconnects from sex because she's confused as to what's acceptable and what isn't.

Mom may take a different path, never inappropriately touching her daughter, but instead making her daughter her own sexual confidant, sharing all the gory details of her sex life. She makes this area into a friend relationship when her daughter needs a parent, not a friend. Although the Sexually Expressive Mom hides nothing sexual from her daughter, she does not go out of her way to share this information. The Sexually Abusive Mom deliberately shares each and every detail. The focus is on Mom's sex life, point by point, and her daughter has to take a backseat to what information Mom dishes out, like it or not. Mom has just stepped over the line into sexual abuse. No daughter should have to listen to Mom's account of what she did or didn't do sexually last night. An emotional disconnection takes place within the daughter because she's been sexualized at too young an age and can't handle it, so she shuts down the emotional part of her life.

The dichotomy is that this mother can be loving in other areas, for example by leading her daughter's Girl Scout troop or making costumes for ballet recitals. In other words, the Sexually Abusive Mom has the ability to act like a regular mom who has her daughter's best interests at heart. The truth is that her thinking is very immature and she assumes that talking about her own sexuality is just a great way to be a mom. Too bad the message to her daughter doesn't convey this.

An abusive mother can take the form of the mom who drags her daughter off to the ob/gyn for an examination, usually around twelve, thirteen, or fourteen, to determine whether she has been "screwing around" and therefore is a slut. Or she takes her to an abortion clinic to see what that's like. The daughter is traumatized by the experience, especially when she hasn't yet been sexually active. This ordeal can cause her to take all emotion out of anything sexual.

Whatever form it takes, abuse is heavy trauma to a daughter's sexuality. Mom condemns her daughter for something that isn't true, and her daughter is humiliated. This turns a daughter against her mom as she sees that her mother doesn't respect her, love her, or even like her.

Another manifestation of the Sexually Abusive Mom is when she doesn't want to believe her daughter is being sexually molested but would rather be in denial so she doesn't have to deal with it. Most of the time the molester is a boyfriend, husband, a good friend, or a relative, and Mom doesn't want to rock the boat with anyone. It could also be that a brother or sister is being sexually abused and the daughter is aware of what is happening. She can keep it a secret or she can tell Mom. If she goes to Mom and informs her, Mom may flat out tell her she's wrong. The daughter learns she can't trust Mom and thinks that maybe she is mistaken for believing something is wrong with the situation. She begins to doubt herself, setting up a lifelong pattern of not trusting her feelings and thoughts, and her self-esteem suffers. Where sex is concerned, she doesn't trust herself or anyone she gets involved with.

As the Sexually Abusive Mom has blown all sexual boundaries, her daughter is left trusting no one and, on top of that, feeling personally powerless. She believes that her emotions are not valid, so she pushes them away.

Prior sexual abuse shows up in the daughter's adult sex life in one of two ways: she is promiscuous or she denounces sex altogether. She might swing from one extreme to the other. She might have sex with the current man in her life to win him over and then suddenly decide sex is too animalistic for her and refuse to engage. That she's a contradiction is an understatement, but if you understand what she's dealing with inside, it makes perfect sense. Whether she's sexually active or sexually shut down, or if she swings between the two, it's clear that she's not emotionally connected to sex. She lives it all in her head—with a few body parts responding—but the emotional feelings have been left in the dust since childhood.

NINA

Nina was frequently bullied by a group of girls in middle school. On some days the taunting got so bad that she was afraid to attend her afternoon classes, which she shared with the bullies. Nina preferred to skip class and at times avoid school altogether. Finally, the teachers noticed Nina's frequent lapses in attendance and called her mother.

When Nina's mom tracked her down and took her home, there was hell to pay. Nina was so nervous she was flushed over her chest and neck, and that was all her mother needed to see. Mom accused her of skipping school to have sex with a secret boyfriend. "You let him touch you all over, didn't you?" she said.

Nina's mom insisted that Nina go to a gynecologist to prove she was no longer a virgin. Nina couldn't believe her mom was making her do that when she was telling her the truth—school was too stressful for her because of the bullies. Even when the doctor confirmed Nina had not had sexual penetration, her mother insisted that she must have done everything else sexually except that.

Four years after that experience, Nina became sexually active; she went wild and tried everything. She had sex with men, sex with women, sex in groups, sex with people her own age, and sex with people much older. Nothing was out of her range of experimentation. She was going to prove her mother right in that she must be a slut. Mom had said so, and now it was true.

This lifestyle got old after a while and Nina was left with no close friends. She visited her mom often and called her regularly, still wanting to be Mom's little girl. She searched for validation from Mom, wanting to be told that she was worthwhile. She was mixed up about the role her mom played in her life. Nina couldn't determine whether her mother was there to call her names and pass judgment on her or to tell her she was a good and valuable person. It was all a muddle.

Nina was so confused about herself, her sexuality, and relationships in general that she sought out therapy. She is still working through her issues around her mom and is having a hard time staying in her adult self long enough to cut the ties with the mom she grew up with.

The daughter of a Sexually Abusive Mom learns that sexual pleasure is a sign of weakness. She has been trained, by sexual abuse in her childhood, to believe that sex is the greatest tool she has to control and manipulate others. Because she has disconnected emotionally, she thinks of sex as mechanical and something to be used against others. It's a military type of existence for her sexually, and she doesn't want to be involved in feelings when she has a job to do: to use her sexuality to her own advantage. To do this she develops rules to keep her emotions in check and compartmentalizes the different areas of her life.

A sexual rule she might have is that no oral sex may be performed on her because it's too personal, but you can do pretty much anything else. Or, maybe she'll give her mate oral sex, but only if he's just had a shower, and even then the timer has been put in motion because her purpose is to manipulate him and not for both of them to experience sexual pleasure. There is always a sense about her that she's a little girl, an uncertainty that surrounds her as if a part of her hasn't grown up, which is in reality what happened.

WHAT TO DO. If you were exposed to any type of sexual abuse, you have probably conditioned yourself to hold back your emotions. You've learned to bury the ability to communicate to others in a healthy way when you are happy, sad, or angry. This is a normal reaction to have. You have learned that sex isn't to be trusted and the person engaged in the act with you is not to be trusted either.

It is important to bring to the surface any anger or shame you may feel about yourself or sex. Understanding your feelings first will help you nurture the child inside you who didn't complain, cry, shout out, or defend herself.

First, start bringing your emotions into focus in all areas of your life. Be able to accept that what you feel is right for you. Keep asking yourself what you are feeling, and try to identify what emotion comes up. You may have to keep asking yourself, but the emotions will become identifiable if you continue to check in with yourself.

You don't have to do anything with the emotions you experience; you just have to acknowledge them. Accept your experience for what it is.

When you have gotten comfortable with that, next work on connecting the mental, physical, and emotional sides of sex. You want to commit to a goal of concentrating on your emotions by thinking about what you are feeling while your body is engaged sexually. To do this you have to be able to recognize when you are in your mind only, perhaps thinking about what Aunt Matilda had to say the other day or what you have to pick up at the grocery store, and bring your mind back to feelings. Don't allow yourself to have only the mental and physical side of sex because then you are missing out on what sex is really about. Having the mental, physical, and emotional parts sexually engaged means all parts of you are present. Then you can fully engage in sex and have the most encompassing sexual experiences of your lifetime.

Because daughters of Sexually Abusive Moms are subconsciously sent the message that they are the weaker, more submissive one and that their body is for the perusal of the other person, learn to both give and receive sexual pleasure and not see receiving as a disadvantage because it makes you weak. You may need some help along the way from a therapist, but it's worth the time investment to be able to work through what's keeping you from enjoying and expressing the totality that sex has to offer.

Move Beyond Mom's Messages

Mothers of various sexual styles come in all ages, appearances, shapes, financial levels, and intelligence echelons. They can be the "earth mother" type, and they can be counted among the socialites of the community. They can live on a farm or in a penthouse, they can live a thousand miles away or down the street, but they all had a sexual agenda when you were growing up.

Her agenda may have been the healthiest this side of the Mississippi, and then again it could have been the worst, but your mother handed her sex gene off to you like a football. You might agree with her views or you might not, depending on your identification and temperamental differences with Mom.

If you find you are living your sexuality according to your mom's schema and it's not the way you would really like it, it can be changed. Her take on sexuality is not written in stone to be handed down from one generation to the next as an irrevocable law. Our society's understanding of sexuality is ever evolving and changing, and you can change with it.

You live in a new sexual world different from the one in which Mom grew up. Society's acceptance of sexuality has changed drastically in the past number of years, and some moms keep up with this change of attitude and adjust their beliefs accordingly while other mothers stick to the tried-and-true of their day, not budging an inch from what they have always believed.

Most women could have a happier, more satisfying sex life if they could get beyond their childhood "in box" that collected flyers from Mom about sexuality. From a little to a lot, many people have unwanted blocks in their sexuality that they don't even know exist. Looking at Mom and seeing what she believed will help you start on your path exploring your own sexuality to see what fits for you personally and not what ideas and conditions Mom imposed on you.

While old messages about sex often affect our sex lives, your inability to separate your own thoughts on sex from Mom's is not the only thing affecting your sexuality. The issues in a specific relationship or even relationships in general hover as well. Also added to the mix is your value of yourself and your assessment of your worth.

Mom's message is the first place to start looking for answers about your sexuality. You need that information to proceed to the next step, which is looking at what else is going down that funnel and affecting your sexuality. When you've identified Mom's input on sexuality and the resulting effect on you, get your cap and gown on, as you have just graduated and are ready for the U of You. Go and buy yourself some flowers or take a walk through the forest or stroll along the seashore. You've uncovered the sex gene that Mom passed down to you, you've discarded the parts of that gene you didn't want, and have now started to clear out the rubbish from your own sexuality.

Mom as Aging Authority

M artha had a surprise when the grocery store clerk called her "ma'am." When had she gone from "miss" to "madam," she wondered? After this happened a few more times, she started becoming aware of aging and took note of her life and the lives of various older women she knew to see how other women dealt with getting older. She noticed a wide discrepancy in how women handled it. A light came on for her that there were many ways of aging and not just the one she saw with her mother.

Her mom aged quietly, not making any waves, but her aunt Jane was a pistol at seventy-five, still driving and letting the neighbors know when their lawn needed to be cut. A mother of a friend had closed down and did nothing but watch television all day. At eighty, another friend's mother was traveling Europe, staying in hostels, and having a ball. Martha knew of a lady who became so crotchety no one wanted to be around her. At fifty, another was adopting a child and loving every minute of the experience.

Martha thought about Farrah Fawcett, who stripped for *Playboy* when she was fifty, and Yoko Ono, who was rumored to be willing to get naked on stage in her seventies. What a different world it was than the world her mother grew up in.

Not that long ago, women at forty were ancient. They were viewed as having passed their prime and were considered older than

Methuselah. There wasn't much left to do in life but be over the hill. They certainly weren't considered to have any sex appeal—that was solely reserved for younger women.

Martha thought about Tina Turner, who was the legs for Hanes hosiery in her fifties and was still strutting her stuff into her sixties. It appeared to be true that fifty is the new thirty, and women can be sexy and productive at any age. She read about Georgia O'Keeffe, who gained fame in her forties with her large flower paintings and painted well into her eighties. It looked like there were upsides to getting older, and Martha felt that she too wanted to embrace her age and what it had to offer, taking in the differences of her age now than in her previous decades.

Now women in their forties and upward could be incredible if they chose to take that path. They could slough off Mom's aging gene and be whatever they wanted to be. The picture of aging had changed forever, and isn't going to stop.

She read about many women who came into their prime when they were older. Laura Ingalls Wilder published the first book of her Little House series when she was sixty-five, and then there was Martha Graham, who premiered one of her choreographic works at ninety-six. Age has higher limits now, and we can look ahead to many years of productivity if we so choose.

Life expectancy is expected to increase, and the prediction is that the number of people reaching one hundred years old will double each decade. Girls born in the early 2000s will even live to be older than one hundred. Mom couldn't even teach you how to be when you've reached those years, but she's put the gear in motion to age in a certain way. You can change that completely if you have a different concept from Mom of what you want your life to look like. No longer does there have to be a forced choice between career and motherhood as many women are doing both, sometimes at different times of their lives. Watching the world go by from a rocking chair isn't the only option to aging, and this excited Martha. She realized that many women aren't as fortunate as she to come to the realization that she doesn't need to follow in Mom's footsteps and adopt her ideas about aging.

She began thinking about the different decades she had gone through and started looking at women in their twenties, thirties, and forties. There was a wide deviation there also. Some younger women were having babies and being stay-at-home moms, while others were attending college preparing for a career path. At forty, some women were taking care of parents while others were free to come and go as they pleased. She became aware that each person went through life on a different roadway.

There was an exciting and groundbreaking episode of "Sex and the City" called "Twenty-Something Girls vs. Thirty-Something Women" in which Carrie is approached by a twenty-something wannabe writer fawning all over her and asking if she would be her mentor. As if that weren't enough to make Carrie feel old, Mr. Big becomes engaged to a twenty-six-year-old, breaking Carrie's heart. Samantha is betrayed professionally by her now ex-assistant, also in her twenties. Charlotte meets a twenty-something man and pretends to be around his age only to find he has given her crabs. Carrie wonders, "What was the allure of the twenties? Shall we fear these newly minted single women as a threat to our very survival, or pity them as clueless halfwits about to get their dreams dashed and illusions shattered? 'Twenty-something girl—friend or foe?'" By the end of the episode they all agree that they wouldn't trade being in their thirties for being back in their twenties again, so even in a "thirty" decade, women realize getting older is better.

What Mom Taught You About Aging

It's no surprise that Mom had a hand in how you go through your different decades. You saw her age, and she showed you her version of how it was to be done; if her mode doesn't work for you, you have other options.

There's nothing wrong and everything right about being the rebel in the family and deciding to age differently from Mom if her way doesn't fit who you are personally. You and your mother are not the same person, and if you are following her aging passageway *just because*, you are disregarding yourself in that process. You have the opportunity to decide how to take on the world and live each stage of your life in the most fulfilling way.

If your mother let life just happen and gave no thought to how she wanted to experience her different stages, you may end up repeating her journey, again either being like her or doing the opposite, which is the same because you are still using Mom as the benchmark. Each stage of life brings with it challenges, gifts, and limits, and you have many decisions to make along the way.

You decide which lifestyle you will have, how you will parent, whom you will choose as a mate, and how you will handle aging parents, grandchildren, divorce or separation, retirement, and your changing body. You can choose to open doors that appear and to continue to learn more about yourself; or, you can simply keep your eyes closed to opportunities that come your way and stay the same throughout your life. If you do decide to age your own way you can accomplish that if you know the steps to take.

First, look at the following questionnaire and pick out your mother's aging style and see what you may have picked up from her. Decide if you are following in her footsteps just because that's what she did or if that is really your choice.

- Is your mother an "on-call grandmother," or does she always have to check her schedule to see where or if she could fit in grandchildren?
- Does she love playing cards with her friends?
- Is she for or against plastic surgery?
- Is she into high fashion or exclusively sweats and sneakers?
- Does she travel the globe or only go to the corner store?

- Is watching television her main form of entertainment?
- Is she always up for a new adventure?
- Does she love having family around often, or does she want more alone time?
- Is she becoming nicer or more cantankerous with age?
- Does exercise mean good health to her?
- Are close friends important to her?
- Is she dependent on others just because she wants to be taken care of or is she independent, handling her own life willingly?
- Is she able to express her feelings and listen to others?
- Is she an extreme person or middle-of-the-road in politics, religion, or child rearing?
- Does she have a young attitude and enjoy having fun, or is she always serious and lightness isn't a part of her?
- Is she completely focused on herself or completely focused on others?

Now that you have answered these questions, ask yourself if there are ways that you are similar to Mom. Are you repeating her life or having one of your own? You may see that Mom is always traveling, and you might admire that or you might feel abandoned because she's never available. If you feel deserted by Mom you can decide you are not going to do that to your children. Taking the middle road would allow you to do some traveling and still be available to your children when needed. You don't want to just do the opposite because then you are re-creating her life, just on the flip side, which isn't going to make you happy either because you are still reacting to the mom gene.

If you are feeling depressed because life hasn't turned out the way you wanted it to be, sad about your choices in life, anxious because you don't feel like you fit in with the world, or fearful that you haven't done what would make you happy, you could be seeing the aging mom gene in action.

No-Win Mother Aging Styles

Some mothers are old at thirty, while others are young at eighty. It's almost the luck of the draw which mother you ended up with, but your mother influences how you age because you were her protégé. She was your role model in aging with or without your consent because she was the woman who showed you the ropes.

Your role model might be a picture of aging gracefully, and then again that picture might be of her fighting age every step of the way with a scowl on her face. There isn't anything you can do about which type of mom you drew, but you can certainly recognize her patterns—and yours—and change what you see that you don't want to repeat. As most mothers aren't ogres, you may want to copy certain traits, but there are other qualities you probably deplore. The choice is yours, so look carefully at Mom's aging persona and determine what you value about her style and want to emulate and what you would rather toss out never to be seen again. Consider whether your mom fits one of the following five aging styles.

1. The Narcissistic Aging Mom. This mother's daughter is manipulated to fulfill Mom's needs since Mom thinks old age is all about her and to heck with everyone else. This mother may want attention just because she has aches and pains. She may be the martyr and feel that her role is to have the family centered on her. This mom has always been focused on herself, and aging makes her self-centeredness more pronounced. The choice for the daughter is to either become narcissistic herself or be surrounded by others who are.

2. The Perpetual Teenage Mom. This mother lives in the past, always chasing the unfulfilled dreams of her youth. There is no evidence of chronological aging with this mother. Daughters of this mom grew up competing with her, or they may have felt they needed to act more mature than their moms. Daughters of these mothers didn't get a realistic sense of aging, so they had to make it up on their own.

3. The Old-at-Any-Age Mom. This mom didn't get a chance to go through the normal developmental stages of life and got stuck in being too old at too young an age. Because this mom had to take on too many serious responsibilities as a youngster, her daughter was shown intensity as a coping mechanism. Mom was at an extreme, and that produces extreme behavior in her daughter, as she knows no other way to live. There is never a middle ground, so the daughter either strongly identifies with Mom or rebels against her.

4. The Leave-Me-Alone Aging Mom. This mom finally, after giving her life to others, simply wants to close up shop and not be bothered. Her daughter senses that her mother was burdened by having to raise her children and is glad her job is now done. The daughter fears releasing Mom's anger about Mom having to give up her formative years. The daughter grows up with distorted views of how relationships work, as she fears releasing anger in others and so lives her life in her head and has unrealistic expectations of relationships. She either becomes caretaker of Mom or distances herself.

5. The Shut-Down Aging Mom. This mom lived in roles all her life. She was a wife, mother, and/or worker and only defined herself by those roles. Now that those functions are winding down she has no sense of identity and has given up, causing her daughter to feel abandoned. Her daughter now has to treat Mom like a child because as Mom ages she has lost perspective of herself, leaving her daughter with a mom in name only. This daughter lives with negative feelings inside and either acts in roles herself with a false smile or becomes angry and volatile.

I have seen daughters from the same family have different outlooks on life and different experiences, but they all in some way react to their mother's aging style. Some will adopt the same style without question, some will do the complete opposite, and others will make a determined effort to change the pattern. It's not always easy to see if you are perpetuating Mom's aging style, but it's there if you look underneath the superficial level. This chapter will help to lift the veil, allowing you to take a close look at the path Mom took in her aging scenario, making it more visible so you can decide what parts you like and which parts you don't want to touch with a ten-foot pole.

Look at these types of mothers and see which message you received not only from your mom, but also from your grandmothers and maybe assorted aunts as well. Unconsciously, as you grew up you looked for role models in aging, and you saw how the adult women in your family handled each decade and each set of circumstances. You saw how they treated children, spouses, their own parents, retirement, leisure time, and their advancing years. You might even go back and look at pictures to see what Mom, or any older woman who had an influence on you, was like at forty, fifty, sixty, and so on. Are there similarities between you?

The Narcissistic Aging Mom

To this mother, her needs, wants, and desires are all that matter and to heck with everyone else. She may give lip service to others' needs, but deep down inside it's all part of the game she plays in getting her own needs met.

There are friends, handpicked, of course, who look up to her, seeing her as an expert on this or that. She can become totally involved in her child's life, getting kudos from her children and/or her associates for that involvement. She can find a niche at work where she shines, and she can choose a mate who won't question her thoughts or abilities. But, sooner or later, life slows down. Her children now have their own lives, her outside work is finished, and friends aren't as readily available because they also have aged or moved away or picked up other interests. That's when Mom's narcissism becomes even more apparent.

This mother doesn't value her daughter's thoughts or opinions. She might give her viewpoint a nod, but the bottom line is that she has to do it her own way because she's the dead center of the universe and *no one* knows better than she does.

The Narcissistic Aging Mom's self-absorption, which she has been carrying around forever because of unmet needs in her childhood, shows up as neediness as she ages. She needs to feel important and in charge of things, so she will do whatever is necessary to fill that hole of emptiness, as that need is as great as it was growing up. It's simply resurfaced now at an older age.

These women manipulate their children with any means they can come up with, which can take the form of laying on guilt by being much too sweet to get something back, overspending on their children, criticizing them, not speaking to them for a period of time, or playing the victim to elicit sympathy. Any behavior will do to make sure Mom's own needs get met. She thinks she's doing the right thing, as most mothers are not monsters, but looked at from an objective point of view, life is all about her and everyone else comes in a paltry second. Her second childhood has arrived, so take it in stride and know what is happening so you don't get caught up in it.

CAROLINE

Caroline was ready to scream. Her aged mother needed this and she needed that and she needed it right now. Even when her mom asked nicely, Caroline wasn't buying into the sweetness any longer, as she had seen over and over that her mother said one thing and really meant another. Her mom needed to feel important and that meant, to her at least, that people should jump when she asked them to. It didn't matter that Caroline might have other plans or responsibilities—her mother could always play the martyr and "suffer in silence" to make Caroline feel guilty if that were the case. Or she could act put out and even, if she felt it was needed, become mean.

A few times Caroline tried talking to her mom about their relationship, sometimes even blowing up at her in her frustration, but her mother always threw in how Caroline used to be such a nice person and now she was so different. What was really happening was that as Caroline's mother aged and her narcissism took over full force, she was draining Caroline. Caroline didn't have the time, energy, or ambition to placate her mother with her increased neediness any longer.

The only thing that mattered to Mom was herself and the way she wanted her life to be. She hadn't needed Caroline quite as much in the years past because she was busy with other activities, but now that she was getting older and her activities have lessened her issues were at the forefront. If Caroline didn't do her mom's bidding, her mother told her that she was lacking in sensitivity.

Caroline wanted to be a good daughter to her mother in her advancing years, but how was she going to balance that with her own life, husband, and children, she wondered. What she ended up doing was spending more time with her mother at the expense of everyone else so she wouldn't feel so guilty about choosing someone or something over Mom. Soon her husband and children were complaining that she was neglecting them.

She asked herself why life had to be so difficult. She was filling her own need to be a "good daughter," taking time away from her children and husband to be the dutiful daughter, but that didn't feel right either. She wanted her mom to approve of her and she also wanted her husband and children to approve of her, but it wasn't working. She couldn't seem to make everyone happy no matter what she did.

A remark from her friend, who commented that Caroline was always trying to get someone's approval, whether it was her mom's, husband's or her children's, woke Caroline up, as she could see the truth in that. What had been a distant thought now came to the surface, causing Caroline to think hard about how she was living her life.

She certainly didn't want to age the way her mother was and focus solely on her own needs. She wanted to be the best person she could be to everyone who was important in her life. She wanted a happy life from now to the end and didn't want to be overly dependent in any way on her own children or even her husband. The last thing she wanted as she aged was to have her children feel guilty about having their own lives and careers and families.

With support from some healthy friends Caroline started delegating most of Mom's basic needs to others. She told her mother that her meals were going to be delivered, saving Caroline time on shopping trips, unloading groceries, cooking, and cleaning for Mom. She ordered cable television, brought her mother books once a month, arranged for Mom's church friends to visit her at home or give her rides to church, and called her every few days just to check in and say hi. She would visit as time allowed, and she tried for once a week, but sometimes a couple of weeks went by before she could get over there.

This wasn't easy for Caroline, and she had to talk to herself a lot about recognizing and honoring her own needs, but not at the expense of others. Sometimes she put her needs before Mom's needs. She had some good friends who helped her through the process, and although she still struggles with her relationship with Mom, she's getting better at detaching.

The Narcissistic Aging Mom can certainly be a trial and tribulation to her children, and if they give her half a chance to manipulate them, they are hooked into pleasing Mom with no way out. Give these mothers an inch and they take a mile. Some daughters can set firm boundaries and not accede to Mom's every wish, and others can't make the distinction between Mom's needs and their own. Some children are more prone to acceding to Mom's wishes than other children who just take Mom in stride and go about their own life. It depends on the needs of each child.

If you are the daughter of a Narcissistic Aging Mom who feels that maybe you could've received a little bit more love, appreciation, respect, and/or approval from Mom in your younger years, you may be set up for the trap of going above and beyond the call of duty to gain those attributes from her now if you don't recognize her true character.

You can never do enough for the narcissistic personality because she believes the world revolves around her and her needs know no end. There's no you, only her, no matter how disguised that may be. If you don't take notice of the Narcissistic Aging Mom, you'll be caught in her web and the mom gene will be there in full force making one person more important than all others—at your own expense.

What to Do. Knowing that you don't want age—whatever that number is to you—to look like Mom's, you must recognize the signs of her self-serving behavior. Does she thank you for every little thing you do for her? If you pull down the shade in her living room window and she gushes, "Thank you" as if you had just brought her the crown jewels, realize what she is really saying is, "You don't do enough for me, so I have to make you feel guilty by going overboard thanking you in hopes of getting more of your attention." She may also take offense at something you did or said and not speak to you for months, punishing you for what she believes is your misdeed. She's going to teach you to make her needs come first by this method so when you come crying back you'll remember to treat her the way she wants to be treated. Whatever way she chooses to manipulate you, it never takes into consideration your feelings.

You must look at this picture carefully to recognize it because in some moms the narcissism is glaring and for others it's very subtle and hardly recognizable at all, just as in the examples given, but it's there just the same. What you want to look for is how often she listens to your point of view, values the information you give her, appreciates your sharing this with her, and *even* once in a while applies it to her life.

Next you must fix firm boundaries so there is some semblance of where she ends and you begin. Decide if you are willing to do her weekly grocery shopping or pay her bills every month. Maybe she drops in without notice and that doesn't work for you, or she may assume she's accompanying you on every vacation you take when that isn't your plan at all. Setting boundaries with her means that you tell her in a calm voice what works for you and what doesn't, without getting caught up in her reaction. You can do this by simply ignoring what she says and not personalizing it. This is about her and not about who you are, so let her be who she is and you be who you are. You really don't need her approval to live your life being you, so make claim to what you need and stick by it. Living this way you make yourself happy, and because this is your life that is what's important.

When you have your boundaries in place make sure your life is in balance. Having commitments outside yourself provides a well-rounded existence as long as you don't give everything you have to others, leaving yourself out of the equation. It can be challenging at times to achieve this balance, but as long as you are aware and working on it you can face all your years from the best possible angle.

The Perpetual Teenage Mom

In some ways this is a fun mom. She is very concerned with her clothes, runs to get her makeup style refreshed four times a year, is always having an issue with her hair, and is basically "one of the girls." Nothing or no one is going to age her, by gosh, no matter how hard they might try.

Some people get stuck at a certain age emotionally, and that is the case for this mom. She is not able to move forward in many areas. She might have a decent job, she might have a steady mate, and she may have children, but underneath all of that there beats a heart of a teen. She doesn't have the maturity to make wise decisions in guiding her daughter or the emotional ability to give her daughter a sense of worthiness. Instead all the focus is on Mom and her being the belle of the ball—just like teens who are self-absorbed.

If Mom is married she may still be the "flirt" of the family and play up to any man who crosses her path. She may take a vacation away from hubby and act like she is single on her trip, getting as much male attention as possible. She thrives on it, and the more the merrier. It's a big game with her, and she is very good at it. Some husbands look the other way and don't confront Mom's adolescent behavior. Other husbands may grow tired of this behavior and leave the marriage nest, as they don't want to play second fiddle to whatever man is around at the moment.

If she is single, the Perpetual Teenage Mom may still be chasing men in earnest, needing their admiration to feel good. It's still a sport for her, but a more serious one than if she was married. Participating in the dating scene or being involved with a lover or two puts her on top of her game. She loves the chase, either way, of the dating ritual. It's as if she didn't get enough of a chance to do this in the appropriate years, maybe because she married too young, and is making up for lost time. Either that or she was arrested in her development by a traumatic event or the distress of her younger years finally caught up with her and she got stuck in adolescence.

I'm sure you have met someone who is like this. They are fun to be around and have many friends because of their joie de vivre outlook on life. The problem arises when their actions overshadow their daughter's needs, leaving the daughter to feel she has to compete with her own mother or invalidate her and do the opposite. Daughters don't want to compete with their mother in appearance, social life, or with men. Yet, some of these daughters have to do just that. Other daughters compensate by appearing more mature than Mom, leaving them without a mother to consult in their quest for maturity.

Because Mom is more like a sister than a mother to her, the daughter doesn't get to see what is normal in the aging process. Instead she may go ahead and participate in Mom's lifestyle, thinking—even subconsciously—that this is the right way to age. This daughter doesn't get to see age-appropriate behavior. This isn't to say Mom should take to a rocking chair at sixty, but she should let her daughter have her own life without a mom who is in the exact same developmental stage the daughter is.

Moms who go out clubbing with their daughters or who date men the same age as their daughters are not letting their daughters individualize in their own way. To do this, daughters need to date, make educational choices, think about a career, make mistakes and learn from them, and find their personal strengths without Mom being front and center in the middle of it all. Mom needs to be in the background, offering guidance in the form of wise advice, rather than being in the same ring as her daughter. By competing, this mom is relaying the message that Mom is more important than her daughter, and that being the case, Mom's needs, wants, and desires are paramount.

TRUDY

Trudy had a mother who loved men. She had been divorced since Trudy was ten, so there had been a number of men coming and going in their lives. Now that Trudy was a married adult woman she watched this from afar, and the pattern was still the same. Her Mom always had to have a man on the scene to make her feel special.

For a number of years, as Trudy grew up, her mother had one boyfriend whom she spent most of her time with. She finally ended that relationship, and after Trudy left home her mother rented a room to a young man. Her mother always referred to him as her boarder, but there were plenty of snickers behind her mom's back. People who knew her mom also knew there was probably a lot more going on than an exchange of rent once a month.

After that ended there was a married lover, whom she told Trudy all about. At the same time there was a dentist who was Trudy's age that her mom tried to pass off as a friend, without much luck. Trudy knew her mom and her need for male attention, so she played along with her mom's story, but she knew the truth all along. Her mother went so far as to have sex in her daughter's bed with this young man when Trudy was out of town. Mom was the aging teenager every step of the way.

Trudy had seen enough of this type of behavior most of her life, and someplace deep inside herself decided she wasn't going to choose relationships where neither side was able to commit. No sir, that was not for her. She chose the most stable man she knew, who was her high school sweetheart, and married him as soon as she could. She was going to stay married to him forever, come hell or high water, and that way she would skip the revolving men scenario that her mother had running through her life.

Of course, Trudy didn't know how to connect emotionally with another person to have a great relationship because Mom never showed her how to do that. Instead, she thought just being with one man was the way to do it differently than Mom.

Trudy and her husband had a nice enough relationship, but there was no real connection or challenge in the marriage, so Trudy was going to remain unconnected as she aged just like Mom. Her mother was going to flit around like a teenage girl, and Trudy was going to be an old married lady. The sad part is that Trudy wasn't going to be able to experience her mature years as she could have without her mom gene of disconnection. It looked different, but she and her mom had one and the same life. They both were shut down to intimacy and aging in the exact same way although they were acting it out differently.

Her mother had damaged Trudy's perspective of aging by her inability to change and mature through each decade. Expectations and responsibilities change in relationships as they go through their different stages, and since she wasn't privy to this maturity from her mom Trudy didn't know how to express her feelings to her husband about him losing his job, making her the breadwinner for a while, or having him retire and be underfoot all day.

All Trudy knew was to do it her mom's way and act like a kid and live a self-centered life or do the total opposite and swallow her feelings and act like everything was just fine. There's that black-and-white thinking once again. The gray area in between could look a bit more balanced with Trudy choosing a man who had a zest for life and a need for intimacy and communication. Sure, that was going to take some work, but look at the rewards it would bring. There would be the chance to age differently than her mom was doing.

If Trudy could see the similarities between her and her mother's lack of intimacy in their lives she could go on to age differently than her mom. If she could see that her mother's actions proved Mom was operating under the illusion that her needs were the most important, Trudy could see she might be doing the same thing *or* making other people's needs more valued than hers.

In her mother's modus operandi *someone's* needs had to be the most significant, so Trudy was never shown flexibility in a mate's needs being important at a given time and have that change to be hers at another time. Once she sees the give-and-take in life she will have the freedom to experience and embrace the changes and advantages of getting older. She will learn to flow with life and take it as it comes, dealing with each age and stage knowing she can adjust to whatever life throws her way. She can be content in that knowledge and not hang on to a prescribed notion that life is either black or white with nothing in between. There's a whole new world as the years pass, but to participate in this newness you have to have cleared up the past messages on aging that Mom handed off to you.

Daughters of Perpetual Teenage Moms can feel like they need to compete with Mom and have the best boyfriend, the best car, the most successful career, and the most wonderful children—better than Mom ever could. They have been competing with Mom since they were teenagers, and it hasn't stopped yet.

Some daughters of this type of mom skip the competing part and act more mature than they really are. They are willing to do anything to be different from Mom, so they become old at a young age.

Imagine what such a daughter's aging process is going to look like. It's very likely she will just get older and older and not have any enjoyment from life because she never learned how to do that in a mature way.

For either daughter of the Perpetual Teenage Mom, it was one way or the other—you either carried on Mom's gene of acting like a teen or you tried to fight it off by doing the opposite, which kept you linked to it also. These daughters may look successful on the outside, but on the inside life is a struggle with them settling for relationships that aren't really satisfying, not getting the full pleasure from work that they could, and having unrealistic expectations of their children because too much or too little is expected of them. These daughters would rather have security and stability in their lives than be Mom's clone. They don't want to be a teen forever, but they always feel that something is missing in their lives.

What to Do. If you had or even still have the Perpetual Teenage Mom, take note from Trudy and look at your life and what you are doing with it. See if you are leading a similar life to Mom or if you have gone to the exact opposite of the spectrum, which is in defiance of Mom's way, so therefore just as influenced by it. Look around at how other women age and ask yourself if that seems to more closely fit your goals, personality, and temperament. Realize you don't have to compete with anyone and you don't have to be overly responsible. Instead, decide to try life a little differently and be just who you are.

Make a list of what's not working to your satisfaction in life. Maybe you want to feel more secure or find a different job. Perhaps you want to relate to your children differently or have a better connection with your partner. All these are possible with an awareness of what your main goal is, the mom gene you are working against, and a desire to live life differently.

Think about what experiences you would like to have in the following areas and write down what you want your life to look like in the coming years.

- Motherhood
- Being a grandmother
- Retirement
- Sex
- Friendships
- Marriage or being single

Read your list every so often and always keep it in mind. Do what you can to bring this picture to life in your world. If you want to travel some day, attend travel seminars, talk to others who travel now, and read about the places you want to visit. If you want to meet new people and expand your social horizons, start volunteering in something that interests you or join a book club; anything new that gets you around others will work to your advantage. If you have a poor body image, go to the gym, take up jogging, or engage in any physical activity that interests you and changes the way you look. Think about your retirement plans and decide how you are going to get to that place. If you are without a mate, consider if you would marry or remarry or would enjoy being alone rather than have a marriage just like your mom.

If you want to feel more secure in your relationships, take more risks with your spouse, stretch your wings, and do something for the both of you that you will be proud of. If your relationship needs some work, you can recognize that you don't need to be resigned to your marriage and accept it the way it is just because you're older or the relationship is older. Getting older means getting better, so make your relationship better by attending some couples seminars or seeing a therapist for a checkup. If you want to understand and relate to your children in a different manner than your mom did with you, it's important to really listen to your children and to learn everything you can about kids and their development. By changing your life now your future will look different. Aging can be a wonderful and beautiful experience, but only if you have decided to do it on your terms in your own way.

The Old-at-Any-Age Mom

This type of mother never got to be a young lady. She got stuck, for a variety of reasons, in being too old at too young an age. You can look at photos and see if she has always had an old, haggard, or serious look about her no matter what her age. Perhaps she had to be the caregiver for her siblings or was a parent at a very young age, or maybe she had to go to work at a young age and juggle home and work life.

Whatever the reason, the Old-at-Any-Age Mom has one side to her, and that doesn't include fun and games. She can go out and have fun once in a while, but there still lurks within her the seriousness of life. She can never let that go for long. She's overresponsible in all areas of her life—never returning a movie or library book late, always being on time, if not early, for everything, has dinner on the table at exactly 6:00 P.M. every single day, goes in to work unless she absolutely can't raise her head off her pillow, or religiously cleans the house every Saturday before she will allow herself something she enjoys. She ages in the same serious manner.

She may be overinvolved with you, overtly casting a disapproving eye when you aren't acting "old enough" by her standards, letting you know you somehow aren't measuring up. She could also be a mom who keeps her distance from you because she's tired and wants to just handle her own life now, but the covert message from her to you in your growing-up years was one of having to accept all responsibilities *and then some* to be a productive member of society. That's her take on life, anyway, and she was or is always there with a negative critique about how you are dealing with life.

Growing older and hopefully wiser throughout the years means you have to accept each chapter in your life for what it is and enjoy it. In your twenties you have a certain perspective on life, which is going to be different than your perspective at fifty. Growing as an adult means you change your outlook and interaction with the world around you. You don't have to give up the basic you, but you do need to keep readjusting and accepting yourself at every age. This is something the Old-at-Any-Age Mom is not equipped to do.

She stays the same "old" mom whatever her age may be. She's stuck there and won't budge. She doesn't describe herself that way, of course, but if you study her closely you can see this theme crop up time after time. The detriment to you as a daughter could be a disconnection with your life, spouse, children, or work, or it could show up in self-sabotage or even in health matters. You could feel out-of-synch with yourself, depressed, anxious, or have a general dissatisfaction with your life.

VICTORIA

Victoria was the baby of the family. She grew up with an Old-at-Any-Age Mom, and observing what that brought her mom, knew that she didn't want that in her life. She wanted some fun, lots of fun to make up for her serious childhood. She didn't want to spend her time washing and cleaning and tending to other people, but rather she wanted the brass ring in the form of having a carefree life.

She met a man who on the outside was extremely extroverted, and his life was centered on having a good time. He would drive down the street in his convertible and wave and yell at other cars like he knew the people inside. He would take Victoria to clubs where they would dance, laugh, and be the life of the party. She loved her life, and she thought she loved this man for saving her from the doldrums of her childhood.

When they had a child, every Sunday morning was theirs and the child knew not to bother them as they slept in, recuperating from their Saturday night out, which was still on their schedule, child or not. At noon they would leave their bed and be ready for the world once again, but until then their child was left to her own devices, feeling not very important and certainly not cared about.

This idealistic life that Victoria thought she had all of a sudden blew up when her daughter was caught buying drugs and she discovered her husband had a gambling addiction and most of their savings were gone. Her daughter was facing legal consequences, and Victoria's life was falling apart. Her daughter was on a self-destructive path, her husband wasn't who she thought he was, and Victoria couldn't figure out where she had gone wrong. Here she had thought she was a fun, happy person, choosing a high-spirited husband and having a daughter who would surely appreciate this lifestyle because it was so different from her own mother's too-serious one, but it seemed to have backfired on her. She had been bound and determined to outwit her mom gene and so lived her life the opposite of Mom's, but her daughter was paying the price by being relegated to the backseat, just as Victoria herself was paying the price of her mom's seriousness. In neither case was there concern for what the daughter needed, but only for the way Mom thought it should be done.

Victoria didn't have realistic expectations of what a balanced life looked like or how it was lived, so she did the opposite of her mom for a few years, then all of a sudden it boomeranged and returned to exactly what she had known growing up. Life indeed was serious, at least to her way of thinking now, and she came to accept that what she had once tried to escape from was really what life was about, part and parcel.

Since the Old-at-Any-Age Mom displays extreme ideologies and behavior, her daughter goes to an extreme also, which is a reactionary response to Mom's way of aging. There is never a middle ground for mom or daughter, so daughters either identify with or rebel against Mom. If a daughter identifies with Mom she's stuck in an overconscientious way of dealing with people and situations, never able to enjoy the lightness of life, and if she rebels against Mom she's set herself up to overemphasize fun at the expense of seeing life and situations realistically. If it isn't fun, she isn't interested, or even aware that there are many facets to all situations.

Neither the too-old daughter nor the rebel has the ability to see the whole picture and experience a balanced life. Without a realistic perspective, life is limited, as these daughters cannot adjust to or accept people and situations that differ from their point of view. They wind up living in a very small world just as their moms did.

What to Do. Start by assessing your self-image. In each of the following categories rate your level of confidence on a scale of 1 to 10, with 1 being less and 10 being more confident.

Sensitivity
Attractiveness
Caring
Determination
Compassion
Sense of humor

Versatility
Flexibility
Empathy
Intelligence
Organization
Body image
Cleverness
Financial savvy
Relationship skills
Positive attitude
Successes and failures

Now think about the areas of your life including relationships, work, family, and friends and identify which areas and behaviors of yours you want to improve. The next step is to prioritize these areas by deciding which are the most important to you in your life right now or where you first want to see changes. Some of the lower rankings in your self-assessment may be acceptable to you, such as being financially savvy when you are fine where you are, or if you see your organizational skills could be improved but don't see the need to develop them as it wouldn't change your life. Choose the ones that have meaning for you and would increase your self-esteem, allowing you to have a happier, more balanced life. See if you and Mom have some of the same threads and determine if your weak points are directly related to the mom gene.

If they are related, you have internalized her negative messages about you and now need to rid yourself of her opinion, replacing it with your own positive image. To do this you must cancel out that voice in your head that says you are "less than."

The way to do that is to note your negative self-talk on the items you marked yourself low in and catch when it is surfacing so you can stop it. Work with affirmations and replace negatives with positives. If your self-talk is that you don't measure up, substitute that feeling with "I feel good about myself." If this self-negativity manifests as "I'm too fat" or "I'm too thin," turn it around to "I accept my body just as it is and am going to look even better."

Know that you are now taking control and not letting the mom gene interfere in your life any longer. She had her opportunity to support you in a positive way and now, as an adult, it's your turn to support yourself in all the constructive ways you can. You and any carried-over mom gene will soon part company, and you will be a much better, happier person than ever before.

The Leave-Me-Alone Aging Mom

This mom has done her duty with friends and children and wants nothing more than to be left alone. Sure you can come and visit once in a while, but not too often, please. She's been there and done that and doesn't want to be bothered anymore with what she really didn't want in the first place: to have her freedom impeded. She would have been just as happy staying single all her life, joining a nunnery, or immersing herself in some artistic pursuit, but that's not what society said she was supposed to do, so she didn't follow her heart. It's not to say that she doesn't like her children well enough, it's just that it wasn't her first choice to raise children, at least at the time when she did.

Instead of following her heart she married, had children, and couldn't wait until they were grown and on their own. As for her husband, he saw what he had and didn't have in his marriage and so immersed himself in work and his cronies. The arrangement worked for the husband and wife because they had a silent agreement not to rattle each other's cages, but to live as pleasant roommates, each with his or her own life.

What identifies this mother is her anger. She may have kept it in check all of her life, but it's there smoldering under the surface beneath her smile and nice demeanor. Her children have picked up on her anger because any little thing they did that was not to her liking was met with a stern look in her eyes and a no-nonsense response, and so as adults they are afraid of anger or any type of confrontation with her.

They never did, and still don't, push or question their mother by asking her for favors or trying to have heart-to-heart talks with her for fear of tapping into her fury, so they learn to keep their emotional distance from her. She gets to keep pretending to her family and friends that she's a nice, kind person by the smile she puts on her face that doesn't quite reach her eyes because she really doesn't care about anyone else's feelings beyond a surface level, so her children learn to detach. She's kept her distance from them, and they better do the same for her.

This distancing from Mom starts becoming more apparent as this mom ages. Where most moms love being grandmothers, the Leave-Me-Alone Aging Mom would rather see her grandchildren every once in a while, but babysitting is out of the question. She wants to read her books and study the classics, she wants to learn everything she can about herbs, she wants to go to the ocean to sit and meditate listening to the waves. She wants to sip her tea on the patio and decide what flowers she's going to plant next. She wants to make up for her proverbial lost time.

She wants her life back now that she's free of children needing her. When her children went off to college or moved out she relieved herself of responsibility to them. Sure they could call and ask a question or two, but beyond that she didn't ask much of them or expect much to come back from them.

This results in a daughter either withdrawing from Mom, smothering her, or trying to find some balance between the two that will please Mom. These daughters didn't have the mom they would've chosen, if they could have, so they make up stories about Mom, themselves, and how life is. They had to decide, on their own, how to handle their mother-daughter relationship since they had a mom

who was only there on a superficial level, not connecting with anyone emotionally.

Because the daughter of a Leave-Me-Alone Aging Mom doesn't
have an emotional outlet when it comes to Mom, the daughter will
live in her head, burying her despair and sense of being gypped out
of a special bond that others seemingly have with their moms. Since
Mom didn't give her anything on a deeper level, this disconnect from
Mom left a large gap in her daughter's ability to have reality-based
expectations. This daughter has made up a fairy tale for herself about
what her mother is really like and has internal imaginings of what a
mother is supposed to be like, just as she has no sense of reality-based
relationships, but instead has made that up in her head also.

SALLY

Sally thought she was a good person and a good daughter,
but if that was really so, why did her mother send her to
boarding school when she was eight? she asked herself. She
thought she must have done something wrong, maybe even
that she just wasn't likeable. This is the scar Sally carried
throughout her life, which interfered with all relationships that
came into her existence. No matter if it was her children,
friends, other family members, or a mate, she believed in some
deep recess of her mind that she was defective and that's why
her mom sent her away.

Her mother was a cold person who couldn't really relate to
anyone, even her children. She didn't have the capability of
putting herself in someone else's shoes to see how her own
actions affected them. She only knew what was right in her
own mind, and no one else was taken into consideration. She
had been raised by an emotionally absent mom herself, so
didn't have any idea there was a different way to parent. Even

though she might give someone a hug, there was a lot of emptiness beneath the physical show of affection.

Sally's mom had moved away when Sally was just barely eighteen and entering university for the first time. If Sally needed to call her she was there at the other end of the phone, but the distance hindered visits back and forth, which suited her mother just fine. Her mother had her life back now and was going to make the most of it. She traveled most of the year, took up the study of metaphysics, and practiced on the piano.

Sally was truly on her own now without even the semblance of Mom being near, and she was scared. Before, she could pretend her mom was involved with her life, but as the holidays came and went with her mom busy someplace or other, Sally sank into a depression. It felt to Sally that indeed she had no worth, as her own mother didn't even value her enough to want to be around for important occasions.

Sally finally met a man, and she married him as fast as she could. He was financially successful and bought Sally whatever she wanted. For a while Sally was happy as she felt this was what she had been looking for all her life. Soon, though, Sally began to have misgivings about her marriage. It seemed that her husband was more concerned with style than substance. She was expected to host dinner parties and attend charity events so he would look good to his associates.

This wasn't the way Sally had envisioned her life, and there were faint rumblings inside telling her that this wasn't much different than what she had grown up with. She had absolutely no emotional connection with her husband and realized how similar that was to her empty relationship with her mother. The cast of characters had changed, but the dynamics were the same. It was as if Sally had married her mother.

Sally's lack of self-esteem, coupled with her husband's emotional detachment from her, made her age the way her mother had—withdrawing from the emotional demands of any relationship, and it showed up in her parenting style.

Sally and her husband had two boys, and she had wanted to be a different type of parent to her children than her mother had been. She tried taking them places and helping them with their homework, but she didn't have an emotional connection to them. When her son came into the living room wearing an outfit she didn't approve of, she criticized him. She told him that she wasn't going to buy him any more clothes if he wasn't going to put the outfits together correctly, continuing down the same path as her mother with the same lack of caring about his feelings, making him feel worthless just as Sally's mom had made her feel.

Sally decided this was all too much work, so she slowly began to withdraw from intimate contact with anyone. On the surface she was the same, but a light had gone out inside of her. She was starting down the same road of aging as her mother. Sally was depressed, and she took it out on her family by detaching from her sons. For Sally, she felt that getting older was easier if she wasn't "bothered." She had unconsciously adopted the aging style of her mother.

One daughter of a Leave-Me-Alone Aging Mom may completely detach from Mom and go about life apart from her family, knowing she wasn't wanted in the first place, thus re-creating Mom's detachment. Another daughter may do everything in her power and be at Mom's beck and call to make Mom like her when there's nothing she can really do to cause that to happen. Her mom is who she is and isn't going to change, much to the chagrin of this daughter.

Another daughter may do it halfway, keeping her distance emotionally, but always being available physically if Mom really needs her. This daughter, of course, ends up being Mom's favorite child. The detachment is there so Mom doesn't have to do much mothering or even socializing with this daughter, but if Mom needs something she's there. This behavior reinforces the mother's choice of parenting style because the daughter allows her mother to have her cake and eat it too, and thus proves to Mom that her mothering style was the best in the world. Often this mom feels no regret about how she chose to parent her children. Not so for the other types of daughters. The one who completely detaches is saying that Mom has no value—even though she's doing the same thing as her mom did—so she's going to look elsewhere to try to get her needs met. The message that gets conveyed to Mom is that Mom had no value to this daughter, so Mom, from her side of the fence, writes her off as a wayward child. Mom doesn't want to know she was inadequate in her approach to mothering, so she makes her daughter the one at fault. Other daughters may take the polar opposite view and feel sorry for Mom, so they become her caretaker.

The daughter who hangs around too much, always vying for Mom's love, is irritating to this mom because Mom needs lots of distance in relationships and her daughter is not allowing her that. Try as hard as she might, no matter what she does, this daughter can't make any headway with getting close to Mom. She hasn't recognized—not yet, at least—that Mom can't get close to anybody.

Growing up, all of these daughters learned to live in their heads and make up stories about relationships, aging, and all other aspects of life because they didn't have a positive role model or an outlet for discussing life's situations. Mom had detached and left them to their own devices and imaginings. Because of that their expectations are often unrealistic, bringing them disappointment in many areas of life.

These daughters may feel unwanted, unworthy, and undervalued because that was the message they picked up from Mom because of her detachment. They can have no sense of self and no idea what their place in life is because they haven't gotten any satisfaction from anything they've tried so far.

WHAT TO DO. The Leave-Me-Alone Aging Mom really and truly does want to be left alone, and once you accept this about her you can begin releasing any hold she has on you. You are on your own, yes, but that doesn't mean you are unworthy. Since you had no role model for what you would feel is a fulfilling aging agenda you must find your own role models for the way you want your life to be now and in the future.

If there are women you know and admire, study them and talk at length to them about their lives. Don't live your life in your head like you had to do growing up, but instead learn to talk about yourself. Find a group that encourages communication or find friends who expect you to share thoughts and feelings.

Examine how realistic your expectations are of yourself and your age. Accepting that you won't make the Olympics if you are over thirty makes life simpler. If you are bound and determined to be a ballet dancer and want to move to Holland, the Netherlands Dance Company III only accepts dancers over forty. Learn what you can and can't do with your particular skills and aptitudes, and apply yourself to what you want.

You might also need to rethink your expectations of relationships and family as you age. When you aren't happy with a certain person or situation, ask yourself if you are viewing them through the eyes of the child you once were. If they evoke the same feelings you had as a child, you are reacting from the past and need to reassess them now as an adult. There is a lot of information out there about what healthy relationships look like, so avail yourself of that and make it one of your goals to learn what good relationships look like and to readjust your expectations.

The payoff of doing life as you see fit is you get to be involved with people, situations, causes, or whatever is important to you knowing you are making a difference in your life. Your years can be as productive and rewarding as you want them to be. All it takes is a new road map and deciding to make that turn a right instead of a left. You do not have to be alone in your anger and resentment as you age, as Mom chose to do.

The Shut-Down Aging Mom

Dependency is fine when someone is young. It's very appropriate. But it's a different story when a person is older and simply wants others to do everything for her because she doesn't have a role in life any longer and so can't do anything for herself. In a Shut-Down-Aging Mom's eyes she's a victim and the world is throwing difficulties at her right and left.

Such a mom is not totally self-centered and can take your feelings into consideration, but she truly can't do for herself. She never has and probably never will be able to accomplish that. As she gets older it's as if she is fading into the woodwork. She is no longer a person you can relate to. It's as if she's closing up shop and going away even though her body is still around. Mom's numbing out can take the form of drinking, drugs, endless television watching, eating and/or weight issues, or excessive reading to the exclusion of most everything else.

What happened with this mom is she had roles to play in her younger years such as being a mom, wife, and/or worker. Then in midlife those roles start to fade, leaving her with a lack of identity. She begins to feel that she has wasted her life and becomes depressed. The question is whether she can reconnect with herself and reinvest in life or will continue down the path of emotionally checking out.

When once upon a time you had a vibrant mother, maybe even a Pollyanna, she now just wants to sit and not do much of anything and expects that you will take care of her. She knows she wants you to handle everything, and whatever you decide is okay with her because she has resigned herself to her inadequacies. It's like having another child to take care of, but this time it's not a child who's dependent—it's your adult mother.

If Mom is closing the shutters, her daughter will feel the loss as Mom fades. Mom has abandoned her daughter, as Mom isn't there any longer for her daughter to share and communicate with. Her daughter has lost her mother in one sense while not really losing her in another. There are no memorials for this, but it's as real as death.

The Shut-Down Aging Mom can easily slide into being a helpless maiden. This dependent creature can't quite get the hang of the different cable channels, or she can't quite make dinner as well as you can, or could you please make her doctor's appointment, as you are much better at it than she is. She gets so confused, she says.

What she is really saying is, "Treat me like I'm a child and take care of me. I don't want to live life as an adult, but would rather you make all the decisions so I can just disconnect." This is a difficult mother to see get older, as she seems to be going backward in age rather than forward, and you have to make certain you aren't duplicating her behavior in any way.

You may not have looked at her as dependent while you were growing up, but she probably has had a trace of dependency most of her life, and looking back you can trace the thread to her younger years.

HELEN

E very time Helen's mother called she always started out by saying, "I don't want to bother you, *but* . . ." Anything could follow from, "Would you take me to the store?" to "Do you have any time to call your brother and ask him to call me?" to "I think I've messed up my medications, would you come over and look?"

Helen, in her growing-up years, had seen her mother take charge of situations, but she didn't understand the take-charge attitude came from a role her mom was operating under. In the past she had seen her mom ask a friend to go with her to pick up Helen at the airport in the next town, and of course, could her friend drive? There was also the time her mother sent Helen's boyfriend to the store because she forgot to buy wine for Thanksgiving dinner.

Mom's detachment was there all along, but she was good at covering it up and looking like she was in control. Now that she had lost any sense of identity, she had the television going every waking minute, while at the same time she was reading a book. Her detachment was obvious, and it seemed to Helen the only purpose she served for her mom was to take care of her basic needs. Everything else had been shut down.

She loved her mother and wanted to help in any way she could, but she missed her mom the way she had been. On top of that Helen was becoming resentful toward her mom because she was expected to fetch without much reciprocation. Helen's anger was close to the surface, ready to break through at any moment, and she was fearful of that happening.

Her mother was getting to be more like a child all the time, and you couldn't get angry at a mom/child, Helen thought. Along with the resentment, Helen was experiencing grief for the loss of the mom she had come to know so well as she grew up. This person had the same body as her mom, but emotionally and mentally she just wasn't a mother anymore.

On top of that her mother's shutting down and becoming dependent was affecting all other aspects of Helen's life, and she couldn't carry on this way. She wondered what she could do to show her mom she cared while at the same time having her own life. Helen decided to be innovative and formed a group of women who were dealing with mom issues. She was surprised at how many women there were who wanted to join, all needing to talk about the subject of Mom in a supportive environment. In the course of their meetings these women had many experiences together, from laughing at mom stories they told to grieving with those who lost their mothers.

The support and networking Helen received was overwhelming. She was referred to therapists, masseuses, acupuncturists, and meditation classes. The others told her she needed to take care of herself during this time and only cater to her mother when absolutely necessary, but never at her own expense. There were social groups for her mom, and if her mom didn't want to participate then that was Mom's choice. Helen didn't have to be her everything, they told her.

Helen also found a mentor in an older woman who was in the group, and they got together regularly and talked for hours about moms, kids, and jobs—you name it. It was a two-way street, as Helen was there for her friend also and the conversations flowed back and forth. Helen began to see what it was like to experience give-and-take in a relationship with another female.

She also learned where she was dependent in her own life and started making small changes to affect the projected outcome of her later years. There was no way she wanted to be a mom like she had, and she was determined to stop the pattern in her family. Her goal was to teach her children that all of them should be individual people who cared for one another, but weren't overly needy in any area.

Her idea for a group was a godsend to her, as she is confronting obstacles with her mother right and left. She's standing up for herself and still feeling like a loving daughter. Helen also accepts that her mother does not think her actions are loving because she now knows what's healthy and what is simply her mother's dysfunction. She's outwitted her aging mom gene and plans on spending all her years growing and as happy as she can make them—for herself and everyone around her.

Daughters of the Shut-Down Aging Mom experience a push/pull, love/hate relationship with Mom as she ages. They may still yearn for her approval, and yet she isn't there to grant that, leaving them with feelings of abandonment. The major effect on the daughter is her mom's unavailability to intimacy. She's seen her mother's detachment, however behind the scenes it was, and knew she couldn't depend on her in emotionally intimate matters, so consequently she feels she can't depend on or trust anyone else in this area.

Since this daughter has been trained from childhood to do things for her mother to get her approval, this daughter will assume the role of acting overly positive or accommodating to others to feel liked. She can take up a caretaking role with Mom because she believes Mom really needs her now, so she's going to help her out, all the time with a smile on her face. Of course, underneath that happy face there are lots of negative feelings and resentment that this daughter doesn't even realize she's harboring.

For this daughter there are several things going on that never allow her to be happy with life and her place in it. She has always had to be in role, has never thought about herself, and then rails against this situation. It's a vicious cycle for her. She needs to be needed and becomes resentful for playing in roles and not getting her own needs met. Her life, instead, becomes one big game in which no one wins because she never learned who she was when she wasn't in a caregiving role. This daughter literally identifies herself by what she does and does not do for her mother or anyone else. As she ages, harboring this resentment, she will shut down, just like Mom.

What to Do. What's normal with your mom's aging style doesn't have to be the way you do it. Since normal in your family meant adopting or living out a certain role and letting it define you, what you have to do is go against the family grain and have an identity apart from your positions in life. You may be a wife, daughter, mother, and/or a worker, but you are also a person apart from that and need to find out who that is.

If you are a daughter of a Shut-Down Aging Mom, make it a point in your life to know who you are outside of the roles you play so that as you age you stay connected to your life and to others around you. That way you will stay interested in life and be interesting to be around, and your life will be filled with many happy experiences.

If you are the accommodating daughter, work on letting go of the need to be liked by understanding your opinion is just as important as anyone else's. You can like yourself even if the other person doesn't. So before you act on something, stop and check in with yourself to see how you feel about it and act accordingly. Ask yourself if your response truly represents what you think and feel or if you are compromising your position in any way. No matter how uncomfortable it may be to not please others, go ahead and do it anyway so that you continue to stay connected to yourself, enabling you to earn your own self-respect.

If you are caught in the trap of not putting yourself first or seeking out certain roles, you must first acknowledge that these roles are limiting you. If you are only defined by being a mom, or wife, or a career woman, you are cutting yourself off from so many aspects of yourself. Because you are not in a true place in life, you may be feeling paralyzed by emotions including sadness, anger, and/or anxiety.

Every time you feel any such feelings, ask yourself what is going on beneath those feelings. If you're angry, who are you angry with? You could be angry with Mom and displacing it elsewhere. If you feel sad, break down where that sadness is really coming from. Perhaps the base of this sadness is about your mom's nonconnection with you. Without knowing the true source, you won't be able to properly express the emotions, deal with their source, and get the monkey off your back once and for all. It's a step-by-step accumulative process, so reward yourself with a pat on the back every time you share emotions in a positive manner and choose not to shut down as Mom did.

Understand that the roles you have today will end or change, and be prepared for those changes. Look for special skills you have. To do this, you can ask others what they think your strong and weak spots are. See if you agree. Now ask yourself the same question. You might find an artistic ability or that you're good with children or that you work well by yourself. Whatever you find that speaks to your heart, take heed of it and put some time and effort into honing these skills so that you can live out your heart's desire and not simply be in a predetermined role. You may have to take some classes or just put your mind on what you want to do, forging ahead to that goal, or even reinvent parts of your life. Your personal needs are important, so continue learning what those are. Whatever you decide to do, meeting these needs will sustain you throughout the aging process—the roles won't.

Now, assess your hopes and dreams, both those of today and those dating back to your childhood. Oftentimes, the hopes and dreams you had way back when will give you a clue to what your true interests were before life took you in another direction.

Determine if you have the special skills and talents to realize what you want in life, being realistic about those wants and skills. If you find all the pieces fit, set the goals you want to achieve, and create an action plan to bring them to light. To do this, first list your goals, then determine if you need more education in certain areas, contact any people you need to for help, and make a list of what needs to happen from A to Z toward your desired outcome. Don't be concerned about where this will lead you. The beauty of self-discovery is that as you start down one path you may find yourself heading toward a different direction. Whatever feels right is where you want to continue and see where it takes you. Never be afraid of changing midstream.

What you are doing differently as you age is learning who you really are, so that down the road you are still invested and excited about life and don't have to shut down like Mom. Instead you will change the aging gene she left in your keeping.

Choose Your Own Route

You can age differently than Mom once you have armed yourself with the knowledge of how and why she aged the way she did. Next you need a desire and determination to be just you and not a carbon copy of her. You have been given ideas on how to turn this mother gene around, so practice with the road maps given in this chapter and keep moving forward.

Your future is in your hands now, which gives *you* the power over what your life will look like in the coming years. It's a heady feeling and experience, so enjoy it!

6

Working Your Way Out of the Mom Gene

You've now seen the influence the mom gene has had in your life and want to change the power it's had over you and your life. Just the thought of living your life differently may cause anxieties to start surfacing, leaving you with butterflies in your stomach, unnamed fears budding, and maybe even an eye twitch or two, but you've decided to work through those and live your life in a manner that would suit you better than the one Mom had a hand in creating.

There are steps to take toward this goal and ideas to remember and reflect on while you are in this process of change, so be patient with yourself and know you are on the road of undoing the remnants of the mom gene your mother left in her wake while raising you. With the correct information, knowing what you need to keep in mind, you can do it. Change in any form, positive or negative, takes lots of practice, time, acclimation, and support. You are now on your way to practicing change in your life, the way you see things, and how you interact with the world around you, so read this chapter whenever you are in a quandary wondering if you're still on the right path in your quest for freedom from Mom's web.

If you feel you're regressing back to Mom's old ways, don't be hard on yourself, mentally beat yourself up, and think you can't do it. Change doesn't take a straight path upward, but comes in steps, which will go backward and forward at different times. Remember you are changing a lifetime of thinking and reacting one way, so be easy on yourself while you are breaking the old mold. Changing your mom gene is something you can do for yourself every day, so take it day by day and give yourself a mental pat on the back for each triumphant moment, no matter how big or small.

Awaking to the Truth

Take an honest inventory of yourself and your life and see what isn't working to your satisfaction. Hopefully, by now you've identified which areas the mom gene is still operating in, be it relationships, family, sex, aging, work, or how you treat yourself. You might want to take some time and sit with that information, thinking about what you've learned from this book and the role your mom played in your life and confirm to yourself that indeed the mom gene is at work.

Once you are comfortable with that fact, commit to having a clear intention to change it and give it your sustained attention and consciousness. Awareness is the first key to change.

Ready, Set, Go

Now is the time to start changing your life while this knowledge is still fresh in your mind and life hasn't come in and taken you in a different direction. It's so easy to get waylaid with work, family, children, your mate, or social events and put off doing the work you know you need to do. Make this change a priority and put it on the front burner. Write a down statement such as "I'm becoming who *I* am," and read it every day to keep it fresh in your mind. Other statements you will want to add to that are simple ones such as "This is what *I* want," "This is okay with *me*," "This makes *me* happy," "These are *my* secret goals," "It's *okay* that *she* feels this way," or "It's just *her* opinion," which will work wonders in reminding you what you are working toward. The key is to keep consciously aware when you do or say something that doesn't truly represent who you are and doesn't meet your needs in the long run.

Slow and Steady Wins the Race

Change that happens too fast is merely superficial and has no staying power. Work toward your goal in a gradual and timely manner. You can't change your relationship or sexuality or anything else in a week or two or even a few months, so think of this as a process that takes time. If you try to rush it you'll just end up doing the opposite or overwhelming yourself so much that you can't follow through. Take your time and proceed slowly, but deliberately. Acknowledge every small step you take, and when you put enough of those steps together you can look back and see the accumulation of all of them and see your progress.

These small steps may not look like much at first, but keep practicing them and they will make all the difference in the world. A small step may be, if Mom leaves you a message asking you to call her and normally you would immediately pick up the phone, you wait until the next day to return her call. Or it could be walking up to your mate and giving him a little kiss on the cheek, which you don't usually do, or saying to your child, "Mom wants to play Barbies, do you?" which is new for you. Change is not big behavioral changes all at once, but little ones, which when all put together look like a big change from your old ways of doing things.

There isn't an exact time when you look at yourself and suddenly say, "Oh, now I look seven or twenty or forty-five." It's a gradual change, but if you look back at pictures showing your different ages you can more readily see your progression. It's the same way with major changes in your life, so be sure to stop once in a while and look back at the way you used to be and the way you are now. If you've been consciously working on changing you will be pleasantly pleased with your progress from this vantage point.

Be Prepared for Reactions

If you think change is hard for you, recognize that it may also be hard on those around you, as they are used to you the other way. Be aware of the kinds of reactions you might receive from others, be they your mate, children, parents, coworkers, or anyone you deal with. You may be lucky enough to have a great support system, but on many occasions you might shock someone and leave him or her wondering where that person he or she once knew has gone. Depending on the closeness and trust of the relationship you may want to share with this person what you are doing, and then again if you think he or she would put up more challenges than you want, keep it all to yourself. Your choice here is another growth area, and *you* get to decide how you want to handle it while being as comfortable with your choice as you can.

You are going to feel uncomfortable at times because your new behavior is so different than what you have done in the past. You are going against the grain of what was "normal" for you, so don't expect it to be all fun and games without feeling unsteady at times. You may question yourself, but put your trust in the process and move toward the shaky feelings, not away from them. Being uncertain, fearful, and anxious at times is a normal way for everyone to feel during the process of change.

If my clients don't feel uncomfortable along the way, I know they aren't doing the work that's needed. When we go against the grain of what we've done in the past our new thoughts and behaviors lead us into unknown ways of dealing with situations, bringing up uncomfortable feelings. For everyone, the unknown is always scary simply because we haven't been there before and don't know what it looks or feels like or what the ramifications of our new ways are going to be. If you are making big changes you may be like Chicken Little and feel the sky is falling, but even though it may feel that way, I assure you it isn't. It's just your reaction to the changes you are making.

Those around you will also be uncomfortable with your changes because they are used to you being another way, and it may seem to them you are changing the rules midstream. They may squirm, get angry, pull away, or confront you because you aren't acting or reacting in your usual manner. It doesn't mean that every relationship and situation will deteriorate. Far from that.

What it does mean is that you have allowed changes to occur not only for you, but also for everyone in your life. It's an opportunity for you to grow and for those around you to grow as well. If you decide you need to be more expressive about your feelings and begin to talk about them more, others may follow your lead and talk about how they feel also because you've just opened up a new way of communicating. It's surprising how positively others will respond to the new you. Positive reactions and reinforcement are another sign you are changing—and that's good.

Practice Your New Skills

Each day you must practice your new skills, knowing change is unfamiliar and uncomfortable, but you have made the commitment to heave the mom gene out the window and you are willing to do what it takes to accomplish your goal of having your own life. Following are some steps to ease the transition from operating in the past to functioning in the here and now, leaving the negative parts of the past in the past.

1. Check in with yourself to see what you are thinking, feeling, and how you are reacting to situations. If this is not something you presently do on a regular basis, you may have to do this hourly or at least a few times a day. I sometimes suggest to my clients that when they're through with their day or whenever they find some down time, they review everything that occurred that day and how they felt about it. This allows you to become more aware of who you are by the way you reacted to people and situations, while putting you closer in touch with your feelings.

2. Verbalize your feelings. If you have found that you feel angry, sad, put upon, happy, pleased, hurt, or inferior, make note of those feelings. Let those emotions of yours be important, and when it's appropriate, verbalize them. It's important to express your reactions and not allow them to be judged. If you are angry it doesn't mean you should try that new maneuver you learned in your kick-boxing class on the offender, but you can certainly explain why you are angry, thereby acknowledging your emotion and verbalizing it.

3. Figure out where your boundaries are and honor them. If you have a friend who always calls you with a sob story and exhibits the "Oh, poor me" attitude time after time, and you're tired of listening, set your boundary by telling her what she's doing and explaining to her how you are feeling unimportant in the friendship because it's one-sided all in her favor. She may change her approach for a call or two, but if it goes back to her being a "sob-sister" once again, exercise your right to use caller ID and not take her calls.

4. Take note of how you feel after you've addressed a situation differently than before. You might feel a mixture of "Oh no, what have I just done?" and "Whoa, I did it!" and that's to be expected. Over time the change will become natural and you will automatically respond as the new person you are becoming. By taking note of how you feel you have acknowledged your feelings and can see that you have just taken a step across the line separating the old and new way. It's an indication of the new you and a step forward, becoming a "pat yourself on the back" moment.

5. Be sure to do for yourself. If you want to laze around all day Saturday, do it—and without guilt. If you'd rather be out gardening or shopping, treat yourself to that. If it's a relationship or situation you need to change, don't hesitate, but start working on making those changes. Whether the desired change is big or small you must honor yourself and not settle for less or compromise yourself in any way. Of course, you have to make adjustments for others in your life, but not at your own expense, time after time. You have to find a balance line.

6. Be gentle with yourself and know this is hard work. You are going to fall numerous times in your mission toward a new you, so please don't expect instant perfection. That way of thinking sets you up to fail, and your goal is success. There will be moments when you stumble and moments when you revert back to your old ways, but they aren't permanent if you keep your eye on the goal, so pick yourself back up, dust off, give yourself a hug, and go at it once again. Soon these stumbles will be further and further apart until one day they hardly happen at all. All this because you were understanding and gentle with yourself.

Your Support System

A strong supportive environment is important when you are making these changes, and you can find yours in many different forms. You may need even two or more places where you are supported and encouraged to sustain your new way of dealing with the world. Some suggestions for members of your support system are family members, coworkers, friends, romantic partners, church groups, 12-step programs, a psychotherapy group, or a private therapist.

Explain what you are doing and ask for your supporters' encouragement when you have acted or reacted in a positive way. Ask them for their help when you've missed a golden opportunity to put the new you out there. They can be your cheering section just as you can be theirs in whatever form they need.

Up, Up, and Away . . . from the Mom Gene

You have now made the decision to do away with any aspect of the mom gene that isn't serving you well and are on your way to new-found freedom and a new lease on life. This is a big step you are taking and one that will change your life in such a positive manner that you'll wonder why you didn't do this sooner.

My philosophy is a person can only do what she can do at that moment in time. If she could have done it differently she would have, but she only had the skills, tools, and information she had at that moment in time. You now have brand-new skills, tools, and information and can live life differently than you've ever been able to before. A new way of living and being is right around the corner, and all you have to do is invest the time and energy to make this happen for you. There's a whole new world waiting for you full of positive thoughts and actions, inner strength, and a new sense of your place in the world. It's a feeling that allows you to be serenely confident in who you are, and you are now on your way to making it happen. Hats off to you!

Index